Rethinking Our Story

Rethinking Our Story

Can We Be Christian in the Quantum Era?

DOUGLAS HAMMACK

RESOURCE *Publications* · Eugene, Oregon

RETHINKING OUR STORY
Can We Be Christian in the Quantum Era?

Resource Publications
An Imprint of Wipf and Stock Publishers
199 W. 8th Ave., Suite 3
Eugene, OR 97401

www.wipfandstock.com

ISBN 13: 978-1-62564-291-2

Manufactured in the USA

Contents

Contents

Rethinking What Will Happen

Afterword

Acknowledgments

Thank you Julie Thomson.
Thank you for your sensitivity to those who do not have a Christian reference. Thank you also, for helping me be kind and gentle to those who do.

Thank you Karen Beesley.
Thank you for corralling unruly words into grammatical sanity. My eyes have been opened. What works for speakers doesn't always work for writers. Thank you.

Thank you Judy Davis.
Thank you for reading, correcting, and encouraging. And I especially thank you for keeping my calendar straight. If it weren't for you, I couldn't have done this project.

Thank you NRCC Church Council (and especially Robin Camu).
Thank you for pushing me out of the business of running a church, and into the business of soul-tending, speaking, and writing. I love my new life!

Thank you Denise.
Thank you for sending me away to write and handling life while I was gone. But what am I saying? You make our lives work all the time. Thank you.

1

The Universe Is Changing

A Tale of Three Balls

Since this is a book about rethinking stories, let's begin with one.

It is a simple story, a story about three balls. Each ball is thrown at a different time in history, each ball tells us something about the time in which it was thrown, and each ball suggests how the church adapted to the worldview of its time.

The First Ball: The Middle Ages and the Unknowable Unknown

Thrown in the year 1300, before the Renaissance and Enlightenment, the path of our first ball was determined by the physics of the day. At that time, the world was a frighteningly unknown and unknowable place. Powerful forces were at work all around, forces we could not fully understand. Lightning struck, but we knew nothing about electrons or protons. Women died in childbirth, but we didn't understand the circulatory system. Crops failed, but we could not imagine microorganisms. There were so many unknowns that we developed a philosophy about reality that told us life's mysteries were simply unknowable to everyday people. It was not expected that humans could understand the deep mysteries of existence.

In this world, the path of the first ball, like most day-to-day realities, was determined by magical, mysterious, unknowable forces. Perhaps the ball's path was determined by tea leaves, or broken mirrors, or black cats. Perhaps the old lady at the edge of town put a spell on the ball. Superstition and magic were necessary guesswork for people who believed themselves powerless in a world that was intrinsically incomprehensible.

And the church of the Middle Ages adapted well to this worldview.

Recognizing people's basic need for meaning in an unpredictable universe, the church told the story of God in a way that fit with the reality of the day. The church positioned itself as a powerful agent, able to discern the mysteries of the universe, able to use spiritual power to protect, guide, and inform people. The church gave people access to powerful, religious magic. Celebrating the Eucharist, the priest would intone from the front, "This is the body," or in Latin, "*ho corpus est.*" The poor souls in the back knew something powerful was happening, but couldn't hear very well. It sounded like the priest was saying "hocus pocus," an incantation they took home to use themselves.

To match this pre-Enlightenment worldview, the church adopted the role of guardian, protector, and advocate. It helped people cope in their unknowable universe. "We'll get you to heaven," church leaders said. "We'll say the prayers that will get you saved. We'll read the Bible for you, explain the world to you, tell you what to do, what to say, and what to believe. We'll stand up for you against the wild forces in this dangerous world. Just do what we say, and you'll be fine."

And this powerful, parental, patriarchal church, this "advocating-for-the-outmatched" church, worked quite well for almost a thousand years. But then, Isaac Newton threw a second ball.

The Second Ball: The Enlightenment and the Solid Universe

The path of the second ball was determined by Newton's precise, mechanical, elegant mathematical formula: $F=ma$; Force equals mass times acceleration.

A shift was afoot in the 1500s. A crop of scientists were showing us that things once unknowable could be known. Galileo, Copernicus, and others made significant discoveries, but more than that, changed how we thought about reality. They introduced a "we can figure things out" mantra to Western society. By the early 1600s, everything from the circulatory system to the orbital paths of planets was becoming understandable, and a new view of reality began to emerge, the view that the universe was a precise and understandable place. Descartes capped this revolution, telling us that not only could we figure stuff out, but our whole identity as human beings was our ability to do so (*I think, therefore I am*).

Reality changed. Things once unknowable became simply "unknown as yet." The universe became solid, precise, mechanical, and figure-out-able. A universe governed by discoverable laws and principles took root in our minds. We called our new worldview "The Enlightenment." We could have called it the "We-Can-Figure-Stuff-Out" worldview.

Newton's ball changed everything. Once it did, the everyday world had to adapt. In the philosophically unknowable universe, we needed champions: powerful people able to discern the unknowable and help us out. Consequently, social structures of the Middle Ages were built on a hierarchy of advocates that helped us navigate life's harsh realities.

In the Middle Ages we needed kings to govern us. Commoners couldn't fathom the mysterious affairs of state. We deferred governance to the divine right of the king. God appointed one man and one man only to determine political policy. His was a divine mandate to discern unknowable mysteries and lead us. But when the universe changed we began to believe we *could* figure out political stuff. Consequently, we had to build a new governing system for the new reality. And we did. We called it democracy. Now everybody got a vote, because everybody could figure out politics.

We also had to rebuild our economic system. In the old world order, we deferred economic production and distribution to a champion who possessed divinely ordained economic insights, the feudal lord. But once the universe changed, and we realized that we *could* figure this stuff out, we had to build a new economic system. Feudalism gave way to capitalism. We gave everybody economic access because in the new reality, we believed everybody could figure out economics.

In this new universe, the church had to be rebuilt as well.

So we had a Reformation. No longer needing the church to be our champion, we created a new system in which everybody could figure religion out on their own. We didn't need a hierarchy of advocates to mediate our salvation anymore; we could do that on our own (*sola fide*). We didn't need champions to read scripture for us and tell us how to live. What we needed was a printing press. What we needed was access to the scriptures (*sola scriptura)*, an authoritative document with which we could figure religion out. So we began to rebuild our religion, hammering out a personal faith independent of the pesky meddling of the old world church. The battle cry of the Reformation was informed by the battle cry of the Enlightenment: "We can figure this stuff out!"

And Western society ate it up!

They loved us! People flocked to the church and stayed. Telling the story of God in Enlightenment terms really worked for us. The years after the Reformation were explosive times of growth and influence for us. We grew in numbers and were given prominence, authority, and an influential voice in society.

During those years, we tailored our story to fit in the new universe. Like it, our religion became solid, precise, and mechanical. Scouring the scriptures, we came up with a clearly articulated, highly understandable religion. We determined all the right doctrines, systematized them in books, and congratulated one another on a job well done. We figured out a proper doctrine for God, Jesus, human nature, sin, redemption, and the afterlife.

We perfectly mirrored the culture. We became steeped in certitude, confident we had the right doctrines, and comfortable that we had discerned the true principles by which to live. The culture was looking for dependable answers to spiritual questions, and we had answers aplenty.

And things would have continued right on being so successful, except a bunch of quantum physicists threw a third ball: a teeny, tiny, subatomic ball.

The Third Ball: Quantum Physics and a Return to the Unknown

Our third ball didn't behave in solid, precise, or mechanical ways. Not at all! It wiggled around in ways that were random, chaotic, uncertain, and once again, mysterious. Neils Bohr threw it first in the early 1900s. Atoms, he showed us, the tiny little balls that make up the universe, are *not* solid after all. The table, once the very picture of solidness, became decidedly not so. It is made up of empty space and electrical charges. Sure, a table *appears* to be solid when a cup is placed on it, but in the new universe, we all began to understand that the very concept of solidness is an illusion.

Then Einstein showed us that the universe isn't a precise place either. A ball thrown near the speed of light demonstrates that time and space are not as constant and absolute as we thought. So called constants are no longer constant. They shift and change depending on where we're standing when we experience them. The new universe became unsolid, illusory, relative, and no longer absolute.

Heisenberg gave us a universe that is fundamentally unknowable. He showed us it is philosophically impossible to understand the basic nature of things. We can know where the little balls that make up the universe are, but not how fast they're going. Or, we can know how fast they're going, but not where they are. Fifty percent of reality is inaccessible to us at all times. The nature of things became, once again, unknowable.

In the early part of the last century, these physicists changed our universe. Solid gave way to unsolid. Certainty gave way to mystery, and absolute gave way to relative. Our universe became a vastly different place.

A New Universe; A New Society; A New Story; A New Church

For the last fifty years, our society has been hard at work rebuilding itself in response to quantum physics, just as it did in response to Newton several centuries ago. We're rethinking politics to match the new reality we live in. Fifty years ago, one's political "ism" was precise, solid, and unquestionably "right." If one's "right" was socialism, democracy was by definition, "wrong," and visa versa. But as a fuzzier, less solid universe overtakes our imagination, we are hard at work rethinking how we do politics. In global political dialog these days, many are working to integrate the truths of both democracy *and* socialism. It has become common to question if democracy is right for all nations at all times. These kinds of thoughts never occurred to us when the world was a solid place.

During the Cold War, capitalism was one of the strongest pillars of Western society. It had done so much to increase productivity and prosperity that it never occurred to people that it might need rethinking one day. However, as our reality is shifting, many are questioning even the solidness of capitalism.

The truth of Western medicine has become a relative truth. Today it has to compete on equal footing with Eastern medicine. Redirecting one's *chi* is just as valid a health option as Western drugs and surgery. Likewise, the concept of family has moved from fixed and certain to fluid and situational. We are testing all kinds of social arrangements that would never have been entertained fifty years ago, when there was only one right way to do family.

And what about the poor preacher, still standing firm on his Reformation-era absolute truths? In a world where few believe that any truth *can* be absolute, what is to become of his solid, precise, absolute doctrines about God, Jesus, and the Bible?

Christians believe that the life and teachings of Jesus were relevant in the Middle Ages, were relevant in the Enlightenment era, and will be relevant as the quantum era unfolds.

However, the way we *tell* the story *will* have to change. We won't be able to continue telling our story with the absolute certitude with which we've become so comfortable. That universe has gone away. As it goes, it makes many Christians really uncomfortable. As we begin rethinking our story for the new universe, there is more than a little reactionary hostility in response. Of course. It is an understandable human reaction to the ground getting shaky under our feet.

It may be small comfort, but we *do* have a Christian doctrine that can help us navigate this transition. It's the doctrine of the ineffability, or incomprehensibility, of God. It tells us that even when we *felt* confident and certain in our doctrines, we weren't. We never fully comprehended God anyway. All we ever had were temporary, incomplete, and inadequate thoughts about God and our God-story. Once we reorient ourselves to the idea that God can never be contained in any thought we think, the rethinking this new era demands of us becomes a lot less frightening.

Bad Stories Lead to Bad Actions

Human beings are storytellers. Stories are the way we make meaning out of experience. Early in our history we told stories to explain the powerful forces of nature. We made meaning with stories of gods riding the storm on chariots of thunder. To help us navigate adversity, we told stories of heroes embodying the virtue and strength we need to face our own struggles.

Stories give us meaning and either embolden or demoralize us. Stories tell us how to act, what to believe, and what we aspire to become. Stories tell us what to look for in life. And since we tend to find whatever we look for, stories are pretty deterministic in the lives we live. They inform our deepest instinctive approach to life.

The more noble and beautiful our stories are, the better we live our lives. If they tell us we are unlovable, hateful, or corrupt beings, that affects us. If they tell us the point of life is to accumulate stuff, or that the world is a dog-eat-dog competition, our instincts adapt accordingly. If we live in a story where we must compete for status, recognition, acceptance, or love, our instincts evolve to match. Stories inform our deepest instincts.

Bad stories lead to bad instincts.
Bad instincts lead to bad actions.

And this is true of spiritual stories most of all.

Since the beginning, stories have been the preferred way to speak of spiritual truths: stories about God and stories about people experiencing God. Over time these smaller stories fused together into a broader, overarching, capital "S" Story, the Story of God. Spiritual stories become *the* Story of the human quest for something higher, lovelier, nobler, and more beautiful. The Story of God informs the deepest human longings. Our yearnings to transcend hate, war, prejudice, lust, and vices of all sorts are inspired by those occasional glimpses of the Divine that affect us so deeply.

Of all our stories, our Story of God interacting with our souls most powerfully impacts the instincts by which we live.

Consequently, when our Christian story gets encrusted or corrupted, the consequences are grave. When church folk become harsh, critical, or judgmental, when grace and forgiveness do not awaken in our souls, a polluted story is the most likely culprit. When church folk become the least likely to care for the environment, to recycle, to vote for environmental concerns, most likely, there is a tweaked story somewhere inside us. When church people fail to rise above the American deception that accumulating and consuming more stuff is the way to happiness, again, it's probably our story that is to blame.

Bad stories lead to bad instincts.
Bad instincts lead to bad actions.

And the deteriorating condition of our church today would indicate that our story has gotten bad.

Our story is not inspiring most of us to virtue. It is not inspiriting us to live nobly or selflessly. It is not enabling us to rise above our lower, lesser natures, and live on behalf of the weak and vulnerable. It is not calling us to stand against evil with a single voice, together resisting the greed, hatred, or bigotry that infect our national life.

The Difference between Story and Doctrine

One of the first classes young seminarians take is "Systematic Theology." It is how we prepare them to be guardians of the faith. The word "systematic" in the title tells something about the way they learn our story. They learn it as a "system."

After Newton threw that second ball, and we Christians adapted our story to match the new universe, an immediate task was to thoroughly inventory and catalog our scriptures into doctrines. We took a scripture from here, a scripture from there, gathered them together by topic, and created a series of doctrines. Chapter 1: the doctrine of God. Chapter 2: the doctrine of human nature, and so forth.

These scripture based doctrines became our way to tell the story. They outline what God is like, what humans are like, how salvation happens, and what souls can expect in the afterlife. Believing the scriptures told us everything we needed to know, believing in logic and deductive reasoning, we felt pretty confident we had religion figured out. We built our doctrines into statements of belief, canons of faith that told us how things are.

But things are changing. Since I was in school, in addition to Systematic Theology, another class is being offered: Narrative Theology. It marks a new approach to theology, stepping back from a system of doctrines, and speaking of the truths of God through story, returning to the way things have been for most of human history.

A list of doctrines is brittle. When our understanding of the universe expands, doctrines don't have the elasticity to expand with us. Story does. When we are exposed to new ways of thinking about God or our own humanity, doctrines tend to constrain us, and eventually break. Story, on the other hand, stretches wide enough to contain our new understanding. Unlike precise doctrines, stories can have more than one meaning. A story can be understood one way in an absolute universe, and then expand to convey different truths in a relative one.

While Enlightenment era Christians were hammering out a good doctrinal system, the universe was precise. Consequently, if we believed "A" was true, then "not A" was by definition not true. This belief, enshrined in sound, irrefutable logic, was the bedrock of Enlightenment and Reformation thinking.

With this approach, once we figured out an "A" truth about baptism, or salvation, or such, anybody who held a "not-A" view was, by definition wrong. *"I'm sorry. You seem like a nice group of Christians, but we cannot stay in fellowship with you. You believe the wrong thing."* Consequently, over the last five hundred years, we've gone from two denominations to thirty-eight thousand, each splitting from one another because we couldn't agree on who had the "A-truth."

Spiritual stories, however, don't require we divide ourselves from one another this way. It is quite possible to see two very different truths from the same story, and savor one another's insights instead of disputing them. A story is more elastic, flexible, and pliant. A story can adapt when needed.

Another Reformation

The quantum era demands that Christians throw another Reformation just like the Newtonian era did. A central demand of another Reformation is rethinking our story. It is happening, but not without some conflict. As happens when change is demanded, many are resisting the process and getting upset with those who are undertaking the task. My goodness! If you want to see hateful, just look at the Christian blogosphere respond to some of the emergent church voices.

But if we resist this rethinking process we will leave for our children a church continuing to suffer a slow death. If we had been born one hundred years earlier, we could have lived out our lives with a stable worldview, a stable church, a stable story. But we weren't. The universe those pesky physicists gave us is now *our* universe. It is the organizing principle behind popular culture, and it *demands* we change. We *have* to rethink our Christian story. We *have* to figure out how to tell our story in terms our young people understand.

But rethinking religion isn't easy. Religion touches a deep part of our souls, and when our cherished beliefs are challenged, we don't tend to respond well. The religious transition being forced upon us can feel very threatening. It is a truism that conservative institutions are conservative because they have something to conserve. The Enlightenment church had a great run. Things went really well. It is not hard to understand why our instincts run deeply to keep things the way they have been.

Again, rethinking religion is not easy.

During the last Reformation we burned each other at the stake. When Protestants today look back at that upheaval, we see it as a slight bend in a mighty religious river flowing directly from Jesus to today. But for those who lived through it, the Reformation must have felt like starting a brand new religion. The idea that one's salvation was found by faith alone, eliminating one of the church's main jobs, must have felt like heresy of the worst order and worthy of death!

Thank God we don't burn people at the stake any more, but the same discomfort is in play as Christianity moves into the quantum era. Religious change is uncomfortable! We fear that deviating from the old ways will imperil our souls. We fear that if we don't tell the story the way it was told to us, we may corrupt the one and true faith, invoking the wrath of God and even condemning our souls to eternal damnation.

In my own attempts to retell our story, I've been called up for a few uncomfortable orthodoxy checks. Members of my own community and denominational supervisors alike have questioned my fidelity to the faith. They are good people intending only to keep our religion safe, and to make sure we honor God. Tinkering with the way we tell our story makes folks really uncomfortable. I've made *myself* uncomfortable. On more than one occasion, I've anguished over the potential that I am corrupting the religion I so cherish. I imagine the Reformers felt the same kind of trepidation.

When I was young I heard a sermon that profoundly shaped how I think about the demanding change our times require. The minister told the story of a job he assigned his kids in the back yard. They got things terribly wrong and made a hash of the area he had them working on. Looking out the window, he saw them huffing and puffing away, doing their best, but making a mess. Before going out, he took a moment to consider what he should do. Should he scold them for getting things wrong or affirm them for working so hard? "I went outside," he said, "I affirmed them, thanked them for their hard work, and worked alongside them to get the job done properly." Of course. That's what good fathers do.

If, in our sincere efforts to retell our Christian story, we get things terribly wrong, shall we fear retribution from God? I don't think so. The testimony of our tradition is sure. While we cannot contain a full understanding of God, we contend that the fundamental nature of the Divine is Love. The testimony of our faith is that the nature of God is grace and tender mercy. If we get things wrong, the Holy Spirit patiently and graciously nudges our hearts. If we are receptive, we find our way. Punishment or banishment just does not figure into the equation. We need not fear, nor react from fear. Ours is simply to proceed with an open, listening posture. We are safe before our God.

A seismic shift is afoot in Western society right now and the church is behind the curve. We honed the telling of our story to work extraordinarily well in the Enlightenment world, but that world is going away rapidly. The challenge before us is to muster the same courage and resolve the Reformers did, to question things we hold sacred, to ask ourselves if our truths are *eternity-true*, or just *Enlightenment-true*.

In the process, we will inevitably get things wrong. We'll swing to one extreme or another. We'll dismantle too much or too little. We'll use bad metaphors and interpret scripture poorly. And when we do, my hope is that we are as gracious to one another as our God is to us. There are a lot of hateful Christian words being thrown at those reinterpreting our story these days. Who knows if the experiments being undertaken are right or wrong, but one thing can be certain. Hatefulness isn't consistent with the life and teaching of Jesus.

When Jesus' followers were rethinking Judaism, they created quite a stir. Some in the old guard thought the upstarts should be killed for their impudence, but one man, Gamaliel, took a posture that should inform our own approach. He suggested a wait and see attitude. "If this thing is not of God," he said, "It'll pass away like so many things in history. But if it *is* of God, it may just be our salvation, and we should certainly not resist it."[1]

This seems a much better approach than burning one another at the blogosphere stake.

About the Book

A good story always has good characters. In ours, the main characters are God, Jesus, and the human race. The first part of the book will look at these three players in our drama. What is God like? What are human beings like? What is Jesus like? Should we think of Jesus as a deity, and if so, what does that mean? Are human beings fundamentally good or bad? How about God? Good? Bad? Capricious? Even a Being?

After that I'll weave the players into a narrative that will hopefully be compelling for folks in the quantum era. I'll ask what *did* happen, before you and I arrived on the scene. We human beings wake up inside this life and find ourselves carriers of a beautiful, glorious, and divine nature. At the same time, we find ourselves living inside a selfish, petty, and often evil nature. Can we hammer out a story that helps us make meaning of this experience? How did we get here? What does God do about it? What should we do about it? How does Jesus fit in the whole thing?

After that, I'll ask what *will* happen. How does our story end? How will things turn out? Is there an afterlife? If so, is it good or bad? Good for some, bad for others?

But before we can begin exploring any of those, we have to first do some thinking about the Bible, our traditional source material. We could have titled those chapters, "Why Do We Wear Poly-Cotton Shirts?" (since the Bible prohibits wearing two fabrics at the same time). It's pretty clear that Christians pick and choose which sections of the scripture we pay attention to. Who decided which ones we heed and which ones we ignore? What were the rules by which we decided?

1. Acts 5:39.

A Brief Warning as We Begin

In this book, we're going to bump up against some people's ideas of what is, and what isn't, orthodox. That can be a little unsettling.

It should be noted that Christian orthodoxy exists as a pretty wide spectrum. We are Eastern Orthodox and Roman Catholic. We are Protestants of all kinds; Lutherans, Calvinists, Anglicans. We are Fundamentalists and Liberals, Pietists and Holiness-ers. We are Baptists and Anabaptists, Evangelicals and Pentecostals. We are Celtic Christians and we are Roman Christians. All of us have different views of how the story should be told, but over the years we have all identified together as "Christian."

But for many Christians in twentieth century America, this wide swath of belief and practice has been reduced considerably. It happened for perfectly understandable reasons. In the late 1800s, the American church was feeling the same kind of threat the Roman church felt when Galileo suggested the earth was not the center of the universe. Darwin had suggested that human beings were created through an evolutionary process. At the same time literary analysis was being applied to the scriptures, and all kinds of new and frightening ideas were emerging about the origins, authorship, and interpretation of our ancient documents.

In 1895, in response to this perceived threat, a group of people at the Niagara Bible Conference in Niagara, Ontario laid out fourteen points to which Christians must assent to be in the club. These became known as the Fundamentals of the Faith, and marked the founding of American Fundamentalism.

By the 1920s, those who wanted to adapt the Christian story to the emerging science and those who wanted to hold to the fundamentals of the faith squared off in a full-blown conflict: the Fundamentalist-Modernist debates. It happened first in the Presbyterian Church, but soon exploded into all the major denominations.

One group contended that new understanding was not a threat, but required adapting the Christian message. The other contended that if we deviated too far from the ancient traditions, soon we would no longer be Christian in any real sense of the word.

As happens when sides are fussing at each other, the two groups didn't do their best listening. Each side demonized the other and spent more energy defending its own concerns than listening to the other. Each side became a caricatured version of itself, holding positions that marginalized the other more than fostering a vibrant spirituality.

And then in the 1960s the American church began its decline. When it did, the Modernist side of the debate started declining first. The Fundamentalists saw this as a validation of their view, and celebrated a victory of belief. By the time they started their own decline a couple decades later, their narrowed version of orthodoxy had become firmly established in the minds of many Christians. Consequently, today many of us believe that some of the most re-actionary interpretations of Christian belief are in fact the only "orthodoxy."

As we rethink the Christian story, we'll be pushing up against a few of these historically reactionary views. When we do, I encourage you to remember the broad swath of belief that constitutes our Christian heritage; belief that predates the 1895 Niagara Bible Conference. Second, I encourage you to consider our specific moment in history. The relatively new universe we find ourselves in makes this moment a time we *must* see things from a variety of perspectives.

Why Do This To Ourselves?

That is an important question: Why impose upon ourselves the rigor and conflict required to rethink our story? Why do this to ourselves?

My answer is simple. I love the church. I've been in it all my life. I know its weaknesses and shortcomings better than most, but I love the church. I love the community. I love the spirituality. I love our call to better the earth.

But if we do not take up the challenge of rethinking the church for the quantum era, there will be no church to pass to our children. I believe the church is worth fighting for, even if the fight is with ourselves.

Several years ago, I was in my office on a Saturday afternoon preparing a lesson for our church (North Raleigh Community Church, "NRCC") the following day. My notes called for a phrase familiar to most Christians, "the mind of Christ." As I was getting ready to type those words, I had an inner pause, a nudge to think it over. I knew the good church people I would speak to the next day would all have a comfortable slot in their brains for the phrase. They'd heard it before. It was safe. However, in the year leading up to that day, I'd been engaged in many conversations with church averse people, folks steeped in the quantum worldview. I knew that to them the phrase would be meaningless, perhaps even off-putting. For them, another term, "the universal mind," would be much more engaging. It would invite inquiry and curiosity and help draw them into the spiritual journey.

However, I faced two complications. First, my church averse friends wouldn't be attending the next day. The good church folk would. Second, the folks who would be there would find the term "universal mind" more than a little off-putting. To them, it would sound like New Age heresy; apostasy.

But a pretty strong sense of responsibility had been brewing in my soul for a long time. I knew I had to start telling the Christian story in a way the new worldview could hear. So there in my office, I stood up, walked over to the window, breathed a prayer for wisdom, waited for clarity (or courage), and then sat back down and typed the words "the universal mind."

I made the determination that day that I would begin speaking to the people who did *not* attend NRCC rather than those who did. I decided to speak to people who could not access the older version of the Christian story. Within a few months of that day, forty percent of our community left. Most of them were quite upset with me. They felt I had stolen their church from them, stolen their tradition, and robbed them of the deep relationships they had formed in our community. Many felt I had betrayed them.

And I had. Earlier in my life, I would have felt the same way they did.

But there was more going on that day in my office than just deciding who would and wouldn't be comfortable at NRCC. I was also grappling with what it means to be a faithful Christian. If I was going to substitute the term "universal mind" for "mind of Christ," I had to know what ground I stood on to do so. To do that, I had to reconfigure my own understanding of our story; I had to begin the process of rethinking that laid the foundation for this whole book.

The synoptic gospels (Matthew, Mark, and Luke) tell the story of Jesus with concrete specificity. They start off with his genealogy, telling us that *this* guy, walking around *this* real estate, at *this* moment in history, did *these* things. That's why we call their gospels "synoptic." They give us a synopsis of the time Jesus walked the earth. If their accounts had been film, theirs would have been the documentaries.

John's gospel on the other hand, has an entirely different feel. If his gospel had been film, it would have been an artsy one. His account is abstract, with layers of thoughtful interpretation. Having had longer to think about things, the author of this gospel tweaked the story to make meaning out of the mind-bending experience of Jesus. He begins his gospel very differently. "In the beginning," he says, "was universal thought (*logos*)." "In the beginning," he says, "was the Greek construct for thought and idea, the universal mind." This *logos* existed in the beginning, comingled *with* the Divine and was itself an expression *of* the Divine. And then, we looked up, and this universal, Divine Mind was walking the earth with us in the person of Jesus . . . the universal mind.

I love my kids. They'll be having kids of their own soon and I will love them too. Also, I've been leading North Raleigh Community Church long enough now that I'm watching some of our babies becoming adults. I love those young people too. And I love the college kids I meet with who are struggling to frame a worldview that will work for them. I love this young generation.

I also love the Christian church.
I am sad, however, that the two will not share this journey together . . .
Unless we muster the courage to hold our own Reformation.
Unless we muster the courage to rethink our story.

Rethinking the Bible

2

The Bible Gets Us in Trouble

Several years ago, I was buttonholed in an airport by a zealous seminary student hell-bent on persuading me that women should not be allowed to speak in church.

A little background:

There's a Southern Baptist church full of gentle, compassionate people on about every corner in Raleigh where I live. Several years ago when I had this experience in the airport, the Southern Baptists were locked in their own version of the Fundamentalist-Modernist Controversy. They called it "the Moderate-Conservative debate," but it was essentially the same argument that had been going on since the 1920s.

About the time I moved to town, the struggle had erupted locally. The seminary in town had experienced a coup. All the Moderates were ousted and the Conservatives took over. At the very time I was settling into my new town, eager seminarians were running all over town looking for internships and first pastorates. Local Moderate pastors were still disgruntled over the coup, so the controversy was quite the buzz.

Of the fourteen points of Fundamentalism, the one the Baptists were most up in arms about was the inerrancy of the Bible. This was why they were so focused on whether women were allowed to speak in church. The Conservatives felt that the Bible was inerrant and that they had interpreted all the texts on the subject correctly. Therefore, it was clear to them that women should *not* speak in church. The Moderates, and many women, weren't happy with that conclusion.

I had come from a church where women spoke, were ordained, and served as elders as a matter of course. People fussing over this issue wasn't even on my radar. However, when I moved to town, *everybody* wanted to fuss about it. One Sunday I invited a woman to speak. As soon as I introduced her, several folks stood up conspicuously to walk out in protest.

What a pain in the neck!

So I decided that if I was going to be able to talk about the subject intelligently, I should read up. I picked up several books, evenly split pro and con. I thought about the subject for a month or so, and then wrote a paper to give to anyone who wondered how our community handled the subject. I figured it would save me time and grief.

And with all this playing in the background, I was waiting in the Dallas airport for my connecting flight home. I was reading one of the pro-women books on my list. Seeing the book, an eager seminarian invited me into an unsolicited chat. We were friendly, but our time was more monologue than chat. He expounded for about twenty minutes on the slippery slope we started down when we let women speak in church. He waxed eloquent on the Greek word *kephale* and the divine wisdom behind gender roles.

After a while, he had talked himself out. Things got quiet between us. After a few moments of silence, I made a simple observation. "That's got to be a really tough position to defend," I said. "Our whole society is doing everything it can to open doors for women, and we Christians are in the unenviable position of closing them."

In a moment of candor, his shoulders dropped, his debate face relaxed. "Man, you don't know the half of it," he said. "I hate having to defend this position. If it weren't for the inerrancy of scripture, I'd drop this position in a minute."

I felt bad for him. His Christian rule book demanded he act in a way he didn't even like acting. What a shame.

The way we Christians tell our story has a lot to do with how we approach and interpret scripture. These days, our manner of using the Bible has been getting us in some real trouble!

Like me, you've probably heard Christian folk say some awful, hateful things. When they do, they're usually confident they're speaking for God. They've read the Bible. They are certain they have properly understood it. Perhaps these examples are familiar:

- One group of Christians condemns another because they baptize the wrong way.

- A Protestant Sunday school class teaches children that Catholics go to hell because they pray to Mary when the Bible says not to (my own childhood experience).

- After 9/11, Christians cite the Bible to say awful things about Muslims.

- An abortion clinic bomber quotes Bible verses to justify his actions.

- During the Civil War, Christians use the Bible to justify slavery.

How we use the Bible can really get us in trouble.

A Little History: The Bible Gets a Promotion

Where do Christians go when we want to know what is right, good, or true? In the late eighteenth century, John Wesley suggested we go four places: scripture, tradition, reason, and experience. His four pillars became known as "Wesley's Quadrilateral." It was an update from the days when the pope was the single, infallible source for all spiritual knowledge and understanding. At other times in history, we've added two other pillars to Wesley's four: the still, small inner voice; and the community of faith.

When the world is in flux, one of the things that goes up for grabs is where we go to get our wisdom. Reformation Christians were in one of those flux times when they decided to shift their reliance away from the parental church, the infallible pope, and the priesthood. Adapting to the "we-can-figure-stuff-out" world, they were looking for a dependable source to help them on their quest for spiritual certainty, security, and confidence. Finding the Bible to be just the ticket, the Reformers gave the book an upgrade. It became *the* definitive source for our understanding of God, Jesus, and the way things are.

As they made this transition, seeing the Bible as one source among many didn't carry enough juice, so they upgraded the Bible and made it the primary source. The Bible became the timeless Word of God.

Elevated in status, the Bible became the place we found everything we were looking for: answers to life's persistent questions, and solutions to life's nagging problems. The Bible became the definitive textbook to study and search out things most pressing to us. We needed something logical and dependable, so we made the Bible logical and dependable. We framed it in our minds as a collection of propositions discernible through deduction and reason. Our priority at the time was to *eliminate* mystery, so the Bible became our authoritative source for figuring out life's spiritual questions: how we got here, what life means, how to live well, and where we're going when we die.

We made the Bible what we needed it to be: solid, trustworthy, respected, and understandable. We came to believe that in it, God had answered all our questions, each one with only one answer, each answer with only one meaning: the right one, the one God intended when he wrote it. By the time I was in Sunday school five hundred years later, I learned that the Bible was my guide for all of life, *"Basic Instructions Before Leaving Earth."* Everything I needed for a full life was in the book.

The Bible became the centerpiece of Enlightenment Christianity.

This changed how we lived our spiritual lives. Other sources of spiritual wisdom were demoted to second place and scripture became *sola,* alone and peerless for dictating the affairs of the soul and church. Other sources that had once been important for the Christian life became subordinate. Tradition, reason, and experience took second place. The quiet nudge of the inner voice and the community of faith also took a back seat. Other wisdom sources were subordinated to, and corrected by, scripture.

Centuries later the upgrade had become a heavy burden for my talkative airport friend. If he had been allowed to keep *other* sources of wisdom, he could have found his way out of his own dilemma. He could have given more weight to the quiet inner voice, the breadth of Christian tradition, and voices from the broader Christian community. He knew his position was untenable, but his religion didn't afford him the tools he needed to resolve his inner conflict. A child of the Reformation, he had to defend the peerless authority of scripture.

Rethinking the Bible

Many Christians I know have stopped reading the Bible. Their emerging quantum sensibilities awaken them to its limitations and vulnerabilities, things they didn't see in the past. Approaching the Bible for surety, confidence, and answers to questions no longer scratches their itch. Our answerbook approach to the Bible causes us see some things in the book, and be blind to others. In the quantum era, our blind spots have grown increasingly uncomfortable. One quick example: in the last part of this book, we'll see how the Bible has much less to say about the afterlife than many of us assume. It just wasn't an important issue for the early authors. However, answers to our pressing questions about the afterlife are *really* important today. When we impose our need for answers on the Bible, we tend to come up with interpretations divorced from the culture, framework, and intent of the authors.

When we insist that the Bible give us answers to our questions, we tend to make it into something it is not. Anyone who approaches the Bible finds a great deal of metaphor, symbol, and simile. The language of spirituality is vague. However, our quest for answers tends to shoehorn symbolic language into something concrete and specific. Our view of the Bible pressures the ancient, often fuzzy passages to be *less* symbolic, *less* metaphorical.

Asking the Bible to be something it isn't gets us into trouble.

And now, as the universe is shifting on us, an absolute, authoritative, answerbook Bible is beginning to pinch. Rather than freeing us, thinking of it this way paralyzes us. When we find contradictions and differing voices in the text, our sense that it is God's perfect Word gets in the way. When we find ambiguity in our scriptures, we assume it is the result of our own sin or stupidity. It can't be that the Bible just *is* ambiguous! God's Word would not be that way, would it?

Before long we think ourselves incapable of finding the right meaning in the text. Clarity and certainty elude us. We don't understand. Frustrated, many surrender the Bible to others, preachers or professors who seem better equipped to tease out God's right answers. Soon our religion becomes a second-hand affair, mediated to us by those "in the know."

But second-hand answers don't satisfy our spiritual hunger.

When we make the Bible something it is not, we diminish and distort it. In the process we weaken our own spiritual lives. When we reduce the Bible to solutions to life-problems and answers to life-questions, the spiritual journey is reduced to solving problems and answering questions. When we make the Bible a text book with answers in the back, our spiritual lives are reduced to the quest for knowledge and a problem-free life.

But the Christian journey is more than that. It is more than right answers. It is about finding our place in the story of God. It is about being drawn into a higher life, a deeper life, a life that dances to the divine song that is always playing in and around us.

Most of my Christian friends who have stopped reading the Bible never made a conscious decision to do so. It just happened. I understand why. When we go to the answer book but find more questions than answers, more problems than solutions, we figure the Bible must be beyond us. We give up. We simply stopped reading it. It never occurred to us that the Bible just *is* problematic, that it just *does* evoke questions.

Arrogance and Humility

Certainty is the enemy of humility . . . and Enlightenment Christians love certainty.

Consider this quote from historian and religious anthropologist, Heinrich Zimmer:

> The best things can't be said. The second best are misunderstood. That's because the second best are using the objects of time and space to refer to transcendence. And they are always misunderstood by being interpreted by time and space. The third best: that's conversation.[1]

Coming to the Bible, Christians would do well to be suspect of how confidently we speak of transcendent things. The Bible is an account of the human quest for the best things, the things that cannot be spoken. The Bible touches on the nature of God, the mystery of somethingness instead of nothingness, the nature of consciousness and existence. The Bible touches on that which transcends human thought and knowledge. It's an account of people trying their best to talk about that which cannot be talked about.

We could paraphrase Zimmer this way:

---

1. Campbell, *The Hero's Journey*, 41.

The greatest things in life, the divine things, the transcendent things, can't be talked about. They exist in a dimension we cannot access.

The second greatest things in life are our attempts to talk about those things that cannot be talked about. Some of the most beautiful things human beings ever experience happen when we try to talk about and live in harmony with the transcendent. However, in these efforts, we have to admit, we usually get things wrong.

So let us be careful never to talk about the first or second greatest things with the same confidence we bring to third things in our day-to-day conversation. Confident assuredness has no place when we speak about the first or second greatest things.

This, I suggest, is why the ancients encouraged us to walk humbly before our God.

Certainty about the transcendent is arrogance. When we speak of the greatest things, spiritual things, arrogance has no place. The story of God is spiritual. As such, we have no grounds to believe that the conclusions we draw, the doctrinal propositions we hammer out, are beyond challenge.

Most churches start their statement of belief with a creedal statement of some sort: "We believe in God the Father, the Maker of heaven and earth . . ." or something along those lines. My own spiritual community (NRCC), captured by this need for humility, starts our statement differently.

At NRCC, we believe in paradox and humility. On the spiritual path, we just can't get away from paradox. Consider these well-rehearsed Christian paradoxes:

- God is one; God is three

- God is good; God allows evil

- God is all-powerful; humans have free choice

- God is merciful; God is just

- Jesus is fully human; Jesus is fully divine

- The scriptures are inspired by God; the scriptures are the words of humans

The paradoxical nature of these central spiritual truths demands of us spiritual humility. We do well not to become rigid in our religious beliefs, but to posture ourselves with hearts constantly open to deeper and deeper dimensions of the transcendent realm, the heart of God.

Biblical certainty tends to make us arrogant. We don't call it that. We call it "standing on God's Word." However, having framed the Bible as an answer book, it is pretty easy to believe we found the right ones. We have been studious; we love and respect those who taught us the Bible. Consequently, it is very difficult to admit we get things wrong. Unintentionally and unconsciously, we become arrogant. We sidestep the humility necessary for the spiritual life.

Humble people tend to understand more than convinced people.

Flexible people tend to discover more than rigid people.

From the time my children were young, I must have said a thousand times, "Be listeners and learners." The same imperative applies to the spiritual life. We do well to open our minds, our hearts, and our understanding. Humility doesn't approach life with a cup full of certainty. Humility approaches life with an empty cup. As scholarly as our pursuits may be, as many years as we have been instructed in the Bible, the teachable heart comes as a beginner, ready to empty his or her cup when new understanding is discerned.

Humility recognizes that the very foundation of the spiritual life is mystery. We might prefer a tidy world with precise definitions, but the spiritual life is just not that way. The spiritual journey has an order of complexity that can't be reduced to simple, precise answers.

When we come to the Bible, it is good for us to acknowledge that we may not get it. Yes, we find some answers, but we usually find even more questions. Look at Jesus. He answered questions with questions. That's just the way the spiritual life is.

The Word of God; the Words of Men

Why did Paul tell slaves to obey their masters? That really bothers me! Why didn't he tell them to stand against injustice and stand for human dignity?

- Why did God tell Joshua to commit genocide at the city of Ai? I hate that!

- Why didn't he encourage peaceful negotiation and nonviolent coexistence?

- Why does Hebrew law teach parents to stone their rebellious teenagers to death? That's crazy!

- Why not train our children with consequences a little less permanent?

These are irrelevant questions today. Nobody appeals to the Bible to condone slavery, genocide, or murdering teenagers. But why not? If the Bible really *is* God's answer book, why don't we do these things? You see how hard it is to keep the Bible in an answer book box. When the Bible is "God's message to you and me," there is no good reason to dismiss these awful things. When we make the Bible a timeless, spiritual textbook, when we tear it from its historical and cultural context, we are set adrift and we get ourselves into trouble.

The orthodox Christian doctrine about scripture is this: "*Scripture is the Word of God. Scripture is the words of men.*" That's it. That's the party line. It's a paradox, yes, but it's our official stand. Like many of the truths of our faith, we are encouraged by those who have gone before us to hold these two mutually exclusive truths in tension with one another. The wisdom of our forebears was to *not* pin the Bible down with certitude, but to allow our experience of scripture to unfold in "both-ness" mystery.

However, Enlightenment Christians aren't comfortable with paradox. We prefer our doctrines logical, determined, and pinned down. Consequently, rather than holding both ancient truths in tension, we tend to swing from one to the other, sometimes considering scripture to be the Word of God, other times the words of human beings. Since 1895 conservative Christians have come down on the "Word of God" side. Not many preachers refer to the Bible as "the words of men." No, "the Word of God" is our synonym for the Bible. Our vocabulary tells us which side of the paradox we've settled on.

As such, we give unbalanced weight to the Bible's divine nature. Even though many Christians have been taught to reject the dictation theory of scripture which tells us God whispered to the authors what to write, we tend to give it a status commensurate with that kind of magical origin. We treat the Bible as a miraculous book, timeless words from God, delivered to each of us individually.

And this gets us into trouble. All the time.

3

A Bible for Our Children

My personal journey with the Christian church has been demanding. Along the way, there has been depression and elation, certainty and doubt, reverence and awe, disdain and contempt. But through it all, I have loved the church. Many days, it has helped me live from an elevated, bigger reality. Those days have more than made up for the ugly ones. The church has helped me frame an interpretive lens by which to live well. For this, I will always love the church. It is this love that demands I rethink the Bible— or lose it.

During my lifetime, the world has shifted so quickly, sometimes I've felt whipsawed. My formative years happened in a solid universe with absolute, certain truths. In that world, I knew how to use the Bible. I knew it had answers, and I knew where to find them. Some smart people had gone before me and left me a library of books, study guides, and theological treatises. I didn't have to start from scratch. I had access to the resources they left me.

But when my universe became unsolid, un-absolute, relative, and illusory, all those resources stopped being helpful. Once the Bible stopped being a compilation of absolute principles and doctrines, I didn't know how to approach it. In this, I *did* feel like I was starting from scratch. Our universe hasn't been quantum-y for very long. Consequently, while some smart people are working hard on resources to help us in the new world, there isn't as much help as there used to be. *We* are the predecessors our children will reference.

So what will we tell them about the Bible in their new universe? How will we help them find in scripture the guidance and wisdom that will help them navigate their lives?

We Must Tell Our Children What the Bible Is Not

When I'm in a cantankerous mood, I like to bait my good Christian friends. "You know, don't you," I'll offer glibly, "that the Bible is *not* the Word of God." They respond with the obligatory bluster and it starts us talking. I keep things rolling with some questions. "If this is God's very Word given us, why don't our ladies wear hats to church? If this is God's very Word, why do we wear poly-cotton blends? Why do we let people with glasses become ministers? All these things are prohibited by one Bible verse or another. Wouldn't it be better, I ask, if we thought the Bible was a place to *look for* the Word of God, to *look for* the story of God?"

When we tell our children that the Bible *is* the "very Word of God," we set them up for interpretive trouble down the road. If the only view we give them is that of a perfect, errorless book to answer their questions, most of them simply abandon it when they discover otherwise. If we would leave the Bible as a legacy for our quantum era children, there a few things we have to rethink.

The Bible Is Not Timeless Truth, Divorced from History and Culture

We cannot deny how complex the Bible is. It tells us an amazing, centuries-old story about people's quest to experience God, but it was not written by people who thought the way we do. It is not a seamless document, written for the sensibilities of people living in a scientific era. It does not start at the beginning or run through to the end. Rather, it is a hodgepodge of poetry, letters, stories, and a few kinds of literature we don't even use anymore. Together, these disparate literary fragments do tell a story, but we have to be cultural and historical detectives to tease it out.

We must also admit that the scriptures aren't consistent. They are often contradictory. They don't even present a unified picture of God. Over the thousands of years it took to compile our sacred texts, the view of God evolved considerably. In the earlier scriptures, God met with people. He met with Abraham in front of his tent to talk things over.[1] Later, God warned people, such as Moses, not to even look at him, lest they be overwhelmed and die.[2]

1. Gen 18:1–5.
2. Exod 33:20.

Abraham did not view God the same way Moses did, and neither of them saw God the way Jesus did.

And yet, for all the complexity and contradiction, in this evolving record of people's quest for God, there is embedded a powerful story in which we can find ourselves, find meaning, and find perspective for our lives.

Embedded in this jumble are nuggets of inspired wisdom that have a unique capacity to teach us, stir and rouse us, and elevate our vision. Like no other book, the Bible is able to rebuke, correct, and equip us to walk a journey that will awaken us to divine life.

One year when I was still driving my son to school, I bought a couple of copies of a daily devotional book. My son and I did the same reading before we went to bed and talked about it on our drive. In one of the readings the author talked about the Bible. He encouraged us to read it, insisting that it would change our lives. He also pointed out several reasons *not* to read it, primarily, because it is hard to understand! My son particularly resonated with this point. The Bible, it said, was written at a time, in a place, and inside a culture we no longer appreciate.

> It's a disorderly collection of sixty-odd books written over a period of more than 3000 years. The text is often tedious, barbaric and obscure. It is full of contradictions and inconsistencies. It is a swarming compost of a book, an Irish stew of poetry and propaganda, law and legalism, myth and murk, history and hysteria.
>
> [It's full of] barbarities, and often fanatical nationalism. There are passages where God is interested in other nations only to the degree that he can use them to whip Israel into line. The Psalms are full of self-righteousness and self-pity, God hardens Pharaoh's heart only to turn around and clobber him for his hard-heartedness.[3]

Our attempts to simplify the Bible, to reduce it to answers and directives, just don't work. In fact, they do just the opposite. When our children dig into it, discover that it's *not* simple, that it's *not* consistent, and that it *doesn't* answer the questions they're asking, they simply leave it on their bookshelf when they leave home.

The Bible was written by people rooted in a historical time and place, doing things for reasons we can no longer understand. Why does Jesus tell the

---

3. Buechner, *Beyond Words*, 43.

Samaritan woman he'd rather help dogs than her? That is so harsh! We don't get it! Why can't we get tattoos?[4] Even tasteful ones? What are our children to think of that? If we do not give them a way to think that allows them to dismiss things like that, they'll just dismiss the Bible.

Rethinking the Bible requires that we dig into its history and culture, recognizing how different these are from our own. It is not an errorless, timeless book. It is a snapshot of spiritual people working their way through the always changing sea of history and culture. Cultures change. Slavery means one thing in the twenty-first century, something else in the first. Gender roles are one way now, and were another way then. Even the idea of God means one thing now, and meant something different then.

A timeless, cultureless message from God would have been easier!

The Bible Isn't Always Clear

Cultural differences are just one reason the Bible is hard to understand. When the universe was solid and the Bible held absolute answers, finding truth was easier. There was one answer, one Truth, and all we had to do was study hard enough to find it. In the new universe, on the other hand, we need to discern truth more broadly, more circumspectly. Truth that applies to *this* situation may not apply to *that* one. What is true in this season of life may not be true in another.

What a hassle!

Research skills and deductive reasoning are not a big enough skill set for the quantum era. This has always been true, but in this fuzzy new world, it is especially important to learn to discern the season, and the truth that applies here, now, in this time. In our new world it is just as important to be able to discern as it is to discover.

Today's is a much weightier demand. Back when we had an absolute universe and clear-cut answers, finding truth was quicker, easier, and more convenient. We could find a scholar or minister, and trust that he or she had properly studied the texts and properly represented God's truth. It was an easier religion back then.

4. Lev 19:28.

To leave a Bible for our children, we must offer them a Bible with a deep and abiding truth that is worth finding, but that is *not* easy to tease out.

We Can Approach the Bible with Both Receptivity and Skepticism

When we believed the Bible had the answers to life's persistent questions, there was very little room for doubt. That is not to say that we didn't have misgivings. Sure we did. Rather, it says that our religious framework didn't encourage questions. It was a simpler world, with a simpler religion. We needed only to figure out what to do, and do it. There wasn't a lot of wiggle room, nor many ethical dilemmas. There were right answers and wrong ones, and the Bible had the right ones.

But, though it was a simpler religion, it was more brittle as well. Firmly the Word of God, the Bible could not be questioned or doubted. When we're honest with ourselves, we have to admit there's some crazy stuff in there! We either had to ignore the crazy parts, or doubt God's very Word. With these limited options, we either stuffed our doubts or we left the faith.

Try explaining Psalm 137 to your child: "*Happy is the man who takes my enemy's little ones and dashes their heads against a rock.*" Only the sick among us do not reject this text. Yet there is no framework for rejecting it (which is what we really do). Rather than admitting out loud that we dismiss some of the Bible, we just ignore troubling issues. We have no framework for saying to our kids, "Sweetie, the author of that psalm was just wrong!"

The Noah story is worse. A favorite in Sunday school curriculums, it tells us that God killed babies, elementary kids, grandmas, kitty cats, mommies and daddies. What kind of God is that? Sure, he decided not to do it again; but he did it *once*!

Later, Noah got drunk and fell asleep naked. His son covered him up, and for his troubles he and all his descendants were condemned to perpetual enslavement and discrimination. What kind of God does that?

These kinds of difficulties are all over our texts. How could it be different in a compilation of documents written over 3000 years, written in cultures that disappeared long ago, and written for audiences whose values and beliefs have been lost to time?

But when we believe God wrote this book for us personally and we believe it contains every answer we need to live well, we have no egress from the craziness. Again, our options are narrowed to ignoring the crazy parts, or leaving the faith.

Biblical inflexibility is immobilizing. Without some elasticity we can't bend when the Bible doesn't make sense. Without the freedom to question and conclude the Bible is just plain wrong, we, like a tree that won't bend with the wind, will break. We'll simply lose the scriptures, as so many have.

I taught a class on Paul's prison epistles several years ago. I laid out a pretty good case that Paul did not write the book of Ephesians and then asked the students what it did to their view of the Bible if the book *said* Paul wrote it, but the evidence said he didn't.

After the lively discussion that ensued, a minister's wife who was taking the class came up to me and rebuked me for creating doubt in student's minds. She ungently told me that I risked destroying their faith by undermining their certitude. After she finished, I suggested that if they were going to be students of the Bible, they would soon learn everything I'd just said. Without a framework for thinking about troubling issues like this, I continued, they would have no option but to reject the Bible. Flexibility and skepticism, I suggested, actually allow us to keep the Bible rather than lose it.

If our doctrine is true; if the Bible is indeed the Word of God *and* the words of men; if the Bible *is* rooted in history, time, culture, and place; then there are going to be serious difficulties when twenty-first century minds read it. Quantum era brains are able to contain paradox and thrive in the tension created by the disparate ideas that the Bible can be *both* the most elevating and meaningful story we know *and* total nonsense.

Howard Thurman, once dean of Howard University, told a story of his grandmother. She was old enough to have lived during the time of slavery in the South.

> My regular chore was to do all of the reading for my grandmother—she could neither read nor write . . . with a feeling of great temerity I asked her one day why it was that she would not let me read any of the Pauline letters. What she told me I shall never forget. "During the days of slavery," she said, "the master's minister would occasionally hold services for the slaves . . . always the white minister used as his text something from Paul. At least three or

four times a year he used as a text: "Slaves be obedient to your masters . . . as unto Christ." Then he would go on to show how, if we were good and happy slaves, God would bless us. I promised my Maker that if I ever learned to read and if freedom ever came, I would never read that part of the Bible.[5]

I've taught my children that this woman did the right thing. She resisted injustice. She stood for the very essence of Jesus's teaching. She stood on the right side of history, righteousness, and justice. However, she did it in a way that makes many Christians uncomfortable. Her interior sense of divine righteousness trumped her commitment to the Bible's inerrant authority.

The Bible is not timeless truth, divorced from history and culture.

The Bible is not easy.

We must give our children permission to bring skepticism and doubt to the Bible.

We Must Re-Elevate Complementary, Non-biblical Sources of Spiritual Wisdom

During the Reformation, when we recrafted the Christian story for the newly emerging reality, it made sense to demote Wesley's other wisdom sources and elevate the scriptures to *sola* status. However, now that the universe has shifted again, there is good reason to restore the sources we demoted five hundred years ago and give them a more equal footing with the Bible. Three of them seem particularly relevant for the quantum era: tradition, the inner voice, and the faith-community.

In matters of the soul, my Anglican friends tend to focus on three of the wisdom sources in Wesley's quadrilateral. They call it a three-legged stool; scripture, reason, and tradition (they leave out experience). Each of these sources acts as a check and balance for the others, giving us our best chance of finding our way forward by holding each in tension with the others.

5. Thurman, *Jesus*, 30.

Re-Elevating Christian Tradition

When Western Christians use the word "tradition," whatever we talk about next has been profoundly shaped by Roman culture. It is just a historical reality; the way things are.

When Constantine made Christianity the official religion of the Roman Empire, two things happened. First, Christianity's fame, fortune, and following were vaulted forward. Second, the values of Rome and the church became so comingled, it became hard to tell them apart. It may be that the corrupting power of the comingling has had a more toxic and lasting effect than the benefit of vaulting forward.

Some have called it an unholy union.

One of the dominant values Rome brought to the marriage was conformity. The Roman phalanx is a study in uniformity. Each soldier on the Roman fighting line knew exactly what the other knew. Each knew exactly how to handle the short sword in the front row, the long sword and spear in the back. If one soldier fell, the one next to him knew exactly how to step in and take his job. They did everything with methodical sameness.

Roman roads carried Roman governors and bureaucrats to the far reaches of civilization, taking with them the standardized "Roman way."

So when Rome and Christianity married, it was no surprise that the church became an institution focused on conformity. The first thing the new Roman church did was convene a series of bishop-councils in Turkey to decide what the party line would be, and immediately told everybody the official way to believe and act, chopping off the heads of anybody who wouldn't go along. Soon, the "Roman way" was the "Christian way."

And this new "Christian way" could have been fine. Good things have spread across the planet because Christians obsessed over doing things the "Christian way." But it stopped being fine when the church got it wrong. The church has gotten some things terribly wrong. When this happened, "tradition," or "The Christian Way" became toxic.

The Roman Empire stopped at Hadrian's Wall in northern England, allowing Christians in the north and west to shape their faith according to vastly different sensibilities. Celtic Christian instincts are quite different from Roman. It was the instinct of Rome to dominate nature; it was the instinct of the

Celts to live in harmony with it. Roman Christians instinctively imposed conformity; Celtic Christians honored diverse ways of experiencing God. Rome focused on a Platonic, sinful view of human nature; Celts focused on divine image breathed into us at creation. Without the same impulse to dominate, control, and conform, the Celts approached indigenous religions from a different angle. They integrated more, vanquished less.

As a result, the Celts had a different "Christian tradition." There are many Christian ways of telling the story of God, Jesus, and the Bible. Often we only know one. If we would keep the Bible, we need to experience it through the lens of a full complement of Christian tradition. We need to tone down the Roman dominance part and hear the *other* Christian ways to experience the faith. As our Christian-Roman-Enlightenment church struggles to survive, struggles to provide direction to our children, it behooves us to revisit, and inform them of the full complement of Christian tradition.

In particular, quantum era children will need to know about our contemplative tradition. *Lectio Divina,* or "sacred reading," is a way to interact with the Bible that transcends simply understanding it. By integrating meditative technique with our approach to scripture, we become more discerning, an essential skill in our fuzzy universe. Christian tradition offers a spirituality deeper than learning, deeper than doctrine.

The Western church has long been uncomfortable with mystery, ambiguity, and nonconformity. Consequently, many of us only celebrate *part* of our tradition. Much of it remains locked and forgotten in the attic of our faith. But Christian tradition is more than the sin conscious Roman view of human nature. Ours is *also* the sense of God's image embedded in our very natures. Ours is *also* an inheritance of direct encounter with the indwelling Spirit of God, a history of moving beyond certitude to mystery, embracing silence and inner spaciousness.

The full complement of Christian tradition speaks a language many Western Christians do not know, offering an interpretive lens that frames the Bible as a story that can feed the deep spiritual hungers of people immersed in the newly emerging, mysterious, illusory, unknowable universe.

To retain the Bible in this new era, we need the full complement of Christian tradition.

Re-Elevating the Inner Voice

In all the centuries from Abraham to today, only a few generations have been literate; only a few have had access to the Bible. How did those generations live a spiritual life without the definitive Word of God? Were they less spiritual? Probably not.

From the beginning, central to the spiritual life has been the capacity to discern the inner voice of God. Growing up in church, I definitely heard about "the still small voice." However, though it was taught, and though I was encouraged to listen for it, the dominant features of my spiritual instruction were about reading, studying, saying prayers, and listening to sermons. (Of course giving money and serving the church were in there too.) "Listen for the quiet inner voice, and live accordingly" didn't get nearly as much air time.

I suspect one reason the inner voice was deemphasized was because ministers were afraid to let people handle the Divine themselves. And for good reason. People are nuts! We do all kinds of crazy things. With "God-told-me" to justify our actions, well Katy, bar the door! Crazy comes out of the woodwork.

But abuses notwithstanding, we have no choice but to restore to the people of God the power of their own capacity to discern the inner voice of God. When this central spiritual practice atrophies, every other source of spiritual wisdom is eventually twisted into the worst kind of abuse.

Demanding as it is to discern the inner voice well, it is a critical spiritual skill in our emerging, ambiguous, uncertain universe. This essential spiritual legacy is a critical component for those wanting to use the Bible well. The wisdom of the inner voice changes the way we relate to the Bible, and what we take from it. With it, we approach the scripture less to find answers and more to seek the promptings, nudges, and whispers of God's Spirit.

Re-Elevating the Faith-Community

Again, added to the Bible, the full complement of Christian wisdom sources affords us checks and balances in our spiritual lives. And one of the most important of these sources is the community of faith. In community, we find our best chance of discerning wisdom from our scriptures, our tradition, reason, experience, and the inner voice.

Elevating the faith-community is a frightening proposition for many. First, because Americans are rugged individualists, taught from birth to make it on our own. We don't like having people "all up in our business," not even spiritual people. Second, because for many of us, past experiences of spiritual community haven't gone well. Sex, money, and power abuse have been big problems in church life. Authoritarian leaders seem to gravitate to spiritual positions and prey on people's spiritual hunger. It's a real problem.

But for all our instincts *not* to build authentic, trusting, and trustworthy community, and for all our bad experiences and failed efforts when we have tried, humans *are* communal beings. We must keep trying to rebuild communities worthy of a central role in our lives.

Trustworthy community acts as guard rails for our soul, keeping us from tumbling into an abyss, and making really dumb decisions. When we approach the Bible looking for either answers or inner nudges, we can make ourselves vulnerable to all kinds of craziness. Older and wiser community members have saved more than a few young men from a great deal of trouble when they confused youthful sexual attraction for a "word from God." Humans need loving, trusting, community around us. We do the spiritual journey best together, acting as corrective resources one for another.

The Bible is the primary source we go to for hammering out our Christian story. We need to use it well because it contains our story, a very *good* story.

It's a story of Ultimacy. It's a story of love triumphing over fear. It's a story of goodness and kindness and peace coming out on top. It's a story of people energized by the Divine rising above the more base parts of their souls. It's a story of people inspired to rise above the dreary sameness of belief and value imposed on them by their societies.

It's a story that tells us that while we cannot contain the Divine in our minds, like the wind that blows, we can set our sails to be carried by it.

When we gather ourselves into a community to live out this story together; when we hold it up to the wisdom of tradition, reason, and experience; when we interpret in concert with the inner voice; we are able to hammer out a story that really works.

We become a lot less concerned about doctrinal fights, a lot less concerned about conforming to the same creed. Our focus shifts to helping one another live a narrative that captures our spiritual imaginations, awakens us to the indwelling divine, and helps us more deeply experience God.

This is the kind of broad experience that bestows meaning and direction to our lives. This is the kind of experience we want to leave our children.

If we would give our children, or anyone living in the quantum era, a Bible that can take us there, we will have to:

- Tell them it's not a timeless answer book, and it's not easy to understand
- Give them permission to be skeptical about the things that disturb them
- Give them complementary sources of spiritual wisdom to help them find, tell, and interpret our story in a way that gives life.

May we find in the Bible life and light for our souls.

Rethinking God

4

New Metaphors for a New Day

My Daughter: A Story

I could not have been prouder when my daughter Haven graduated from college and received her nursing pin. It was a good year. At the same time she was entering a noble career that perfectly fit her temperament, she was making plans to marry a good man. It was a happy time for our whole family. Our firstborn, a picture of youth, beauty, and energy was stepping over the threshold into her new life, a new career, a new love, and the hope of a family of her own.

But Haven wasn't completely happy.

During those busy, wedding-planning, nursing-school-finishing days, she asked me to coffee to talk about an anxiety that had been dominating her days. My daughter has a deeply compassionate heart. During her nursing school rotations, she had been on the front line, watching what life does to people. She saw people, both kind and harsh, have car accidents. She saw poor and rich alike suffer heart attacks. She saw both Christians and atheists contract tumors. Terrible things happen to people, and in her new career, she was right there to see it happen.

"And what if it happens to me, Dad?" she asked when we met. "I've never loved anybody the way I love Nick [her new husband]. What if he gets sick and dies? What if one day, my kids end up in the pediatric ward? What if our new life together is destroyed by an accident? There is no guarantee that my life won't end up like the lives of the folks in the hospital every day. Is there?"

After she talked through all the anxious thoughts that had been keeping her up nights there was a pause in the conversation. After a few moments I made a suggestion that must have seemed out of left field.

"Sweetie, I think you need a new God."

I'm sure that wasn't what she wanted to talk about, but she is a kind heart, and patient with her father, so I continued. "The God you grew up with has always been 'Our Father Who Art in Heaven.' That's the God most Christians grow up with. But at the same time you were being taught that image of God, you were living in our house where your father here on earth has tried to move heaven and earth to make yours a good life. Every day you work in the hospital you face the juxtaposition of those two 'fathers.' If I were you, experiencing what you are experiencing, I'd probably be thinking that my 'Father in Heaven' must be asleep on the job. He's not doing those things for his children in the hospital that your father here on earth committed his life to do for you.

"I think in your place, I would be having the same anxiety you are. I would be wondering in the back of my mind, 'What's the deal? What kind of God is this? If God lets his children in the hospital suffer like that, what's to keep him from allowing that same kind of stuff to happen to me, or Nick, or the kids I hope to have one day?'"

She quietly nodded.

"Well again," I continued, "I think you need a new God."

We talked about the words of Jesus. A grain of wheat falls into the ground and dies, but on the other side it is resurrected into a new form of life.[1] "Images of God are like that," I told her. "As we grow, the images of God that helped us when we were young have to die. It feels awful! It can be a ripping, devastating process to go through, but on the other side there are *new* ways of thinking about God, new ways to experience Divine Life.

"If you only think of God as your 'father,' you shrink your experience of the Divine. No wonder you are having the anxiety you are. If God really *is* a father, then we have to be honest, he's not a very good one! He stands by while people get cancer, get shot, lose their children, and worse. Horrible things happen every day, and our Father in Heaven just lets them happen.

1. John 12:24.

44

"This is a problem for Christians, don't you think?

"But," I suggested, "I don't think the problem is a God-problem. I think the image of God we carry around in our heads is the problem."

I began to talk to her about the focus of this chapter, rethinking our images of God. I said to her, "Let's set the 'our-Father' image of God aside for a bit and give ourselves some creative latitude in how we think of God. One of the terms for God in our tradition is 'the Ground of Being.' Let's imagine what our spiritual lives would be like if we thought of God more like soil for a plant than a father of a young woman. If we imagine God as the earth in which our truest beings are rooted, it might change how we search for, and how we experience God.

"A different image of God changes our spiritual lives profoundly. If we think of God as nutrient and energy, as the source from which we draw life and strength, it changes our spiritual instincts. If God were the substrate from which we draw being, then Divine Life is always present *in* us, and we are always present in *God*. If this was our view of God, it would mean we always have access to the Divine. It would mean we are as inseparable from God as a tree is from the soil. Like the tree, Divine Life is always there, always surrounding and sustaining us.

"If the day ever comes that you lose Nick to cancer, or your child to a car accident, the promise of your spiritual heritage is that even then, even in the face of the most difficult thing human beings face, even then you can find peace and joy. Peace and joy are the Fruit of God's Spirit, and you are rooted in God's Spirit.

"You are in God-Soil, and God-Soil is in you. If war breaks out here in Raleigh, and we lose everything, even then we will be able to find life, love, and peace; for life, love, and peace are of God . . . and we are *in* and *of* God. If your brother falls off a mountain on his big adventure [Haven's brother was traveling the world climbing rocks at the time], if Mom or I die of a horrible disease, if everything you love is taken from you, what cannot be taken from you is your humanity. And if humanity is rooted in, and draws source from Divine Life, then we will always have access to the fruit of the Divine Spirit.[2] And that, Sweetie, changes everything."

2. Love, joy peace, patience, kindness, goodness, faithfulness, gentleness, self-control (Gal 5:22–23).

The "soil" image of God I shared with my daughter is a rich part of our Christian heritage. Paul imagined God as a substrate in which "we live, and move, and have being."[3] Thomas Merton spoke of God being present as the "Ground of Our Being, even while remaining hidden from our investigating minds."[4] In our efforts to speak of God, "soil" is an image that can profoundly deepen our spiritual experience.

- Different ways of thinking about God evoke different questions about life.

- Different ways of thinking about God invite us to follow different spiritual paths.

- Different ways of thinking about God call us to different life experiences.

Our Heritage of Humility

The problem with rethinking our images of God for the quantum era is that we are people of tradition. Our tradition has taught us about "Our Father Who Art in Heaven." Who are we to tinker with this long and honored heritage of God-thought?

But "Our Father" is not the only God our tradition has given us. Christians have always been at our best when we have humbly acknowledged that whatever our current concept of God is, it is provisional at best. This too, is a long and storied part of our tradition. From the beginning we have regularly updated our images of God. As the Bible unfolded, about every thousand years, we have updated our dominant image of God.

The Bible we have today does not follow the order in which it was written. Today's Bible is a compilation of many documents written over thousands of years, woven together to tell a story with a beginning, middle, and end. Consequently, we often have two texts set next to each other that were written thousands of years apart. This gives continuity to the narrative but sometimes makes for confusing reading. This happened in the first few chapters of Genesis. The first chapter is a poem written at a very different time from the second and third chapters. So of course, the two accounts are quite different from one another.

3. Acts 17:28.
4. Merton, "Modern Spirituality," para. 9.

Biblical historians do a great job of describing the life and times of those generations from which our scriptures come. But even without their help, a cursory look at the scriptures shows how we update our images of God over time.

When we read about God meeting Abraham at his tent to discuss the destruction of Sodom, it is clear the author imagined God one way. His was the kind of God who met with people face-to-face, who engaged in old-fashioned bartering, and who enjoyed some goat for dinner.[5]

But by the time our scriptures tell the story of Moses on Mount Sinai, our idea of God had undergone a significant update. The author tells the story of Moses hiding himself in a crevice on the mountaintop and barely sneaking a sideways glance at the backside of God's robe. Yet even that much exposure to the Divine lit him up so brightly he had to wear a bag on his head to avoid hurting people's eyes.[6] Later, Jesus updated God for his own time. He taught us that nobody has ever heard God's voice or seen his form.[7] Following Jesus's lead, Paul wrote to Timothy and spoke of God dwelling in "unapproachable light," that no person has seen or is able to see.[8]

These ideas about God are really different! In fact, they are mutually exclusive of one another. How can God both share a meal with Abraham, and also cause the death of anyone who sees him?[9]

Through the generations, Judeo-Christians have been pretty pragmatic about our evolving thoughts about God. It has been more important to us that our view of God is helpful than that it remain consistent. Whenever our spiritual ancestors found a particular concept of God constricting, they simply abandoned it for another, more helpful one. The concept of God has been flexible enough through the years to allow us to adapt our story as we had deeper and deeper experiences of God.

Humility about our images of God has been a great strength through the years. Again, we are at our best when we acknowledge how limited our conceptions of God are, when we think of our images of God as temporary and provisional.

5. Genesis 18 narrates this story.

6. Exod 33:21–23.

7. John 7:37.

8. 1 Tim 6:16.

9. Exod 33:20.

Humility about our God-images runs deep. In our Hebrew tradition, we were forbidden to even speak the word for God. We stripped out the vowels so it could not be pronounced (*YWHW*). "Don't be deceived into thinking you understand God," our ancestors were saying. "When you say the word 'God,' an image forms in your mind of what you're talking about. As soon as that image forms, you have reduced God to fit in your brain and any construct you form will be too limited. We cannot contain the vastness of the Divine. So don't even try. Don't say the word. Don't sculpt an image. God is simply too big for the human mind to contain."

With a few Renaissance exceptions, our Christian tradition has generally heeded the Hebrew injunction not to create pictures or statues of God (graven images). In the wisdom of the ages, we are warned not to hold the concept of God with too much certainty, but to leave it in the realm of the unknowable unknown. It is not the Christian way to be too married to any idea of God. Humility demands we see these images as provisional and temporary, helpful for a season, even life altering and transformative at times. However, as their usefulness fades, our souls need to formulate new understandings of the infinite Divine.

So, when you and I have an idea in our heads that says, "God is like this," there is one thing we know about our formulation. It does *not* contain God.

Even those images of God we cherish are inadequate:

- God is our Father; a limited image.
- God is Judge or King; incomplete images.
- Bridegroom or Lover; insufficient.
- Feminine wisdom Sophia; again, deficient.

What Else Can We Do?

Of course, we *do* form images of God in our minds. It turns out to be extraordinarily helpful to do so. Images are all we have. Remember Zimmer's quote in chapter two: "The best things in life can't be talked about." Our images of God fit in the category of second best things, our attempts to talk about that which can't be talked about.

The problem is not that we formulate metaphors or images for God. The problem is that we eventually begin to believe that the metaphor is the reality.

When we begin to believe that God *is* a King, *is* a Father, *is* a Judge, and when we construct our spiritual lives accordingly, we diminish them.

Any image of God we construct will eventually stop working. Like tight shoes or pants we outgrow, our images begin to constrict. It may happen the same way it did for my daughter, without making the connection between our anxieties and our images of God. It may just manifest with an internal sense of trouble. For many, the patriarchal overtones of a masculine God have felt constricting over the last several generations. The same is true of the condemnation overtones of a Judge-God.

When I was a teenager, I was deeply inspired by the image of God as King. I subconsciously imagined myself a knight at the celestial round table. With sword clasped to breast, I knelt before God, my lord, my liege. I committed myself to live or die in service to my King. It was a powerful metaphor, and I am who I am today because it inspired an early commitment to surrender and service. However, I can no longer find God in the image of King. It's gone. Try as I might, I can't get it back.

In the early 400s Augustine, one of the Church's early bishops, wrote a treatise on the nature of God.[10] In it he grappled for pages and pages with second best things, efforts to talk about the Divine, that which cannot be talked about. When he was finished he concluded with this: "We have said this not in order to say something, but in order not to remain altogether silent."[11]

We struggle with language when we attempt to wrestle from our souls something we sense about the Divine; something we cannot fully articulate. We intuit there is something there, but it eludes us, staying just outside our reach. We have moments when we are bathed in divine experience, when we capture divine love and life and goodness with startling clarity. We stand on a mountaintop or watch an innocent child at play, and our hearts awaken to Something . . . Something.

We try to talk about our experience. If we don't, we feel, the rocks themselves will cry out. If we do not talk about that which cannot be talked about, our hearts will explode within us.

God, the incomprehensible, is nevertheless the deepest drive within us. Our deepest longing is to experience that which is not experienceable, to define

10. Augustine, *On the Trinity*.

11. Tippet, *"The Need for Creeds,"* para. 70.

the indefinable. What can we do but grapple with the limited language we have?

But for all this internal need to speak, we are at our best when we do so without the arrogant assumption that our thoughts and words can contain the ineffable Divine.

Talking About That Which Cannot Be Talked About

This long tradition of tinkering with our images of God is especially important now as we enter the quantum era. As the lens of illusion, relativity, and uncertainty demands everything be rethought, our historical permission to rethink our images of God is especially important. In our times, the work before us is to reimagine God in ways that both work in our new universe, *and* are faithful to our ancient past.

During the Enlightenment era our instincts were to squeeze mystery out of our religion. In our desire to make our religion more comprehensible in a precise universe, we shoehorned God into a few static images, sowing the seeds of our eventual suffocation. Those seeds have now germinated and we're strangling under a doctrinal system about God that has become too constricting.

The word "anthropomorphism" comes from two Greek words: *anthropos* (humanity), and *morphous* (having a shape or form). It means to give a human form to something that isn't human. In religion, it points to our tendency to project human characteristics onto God. We get angry, so we assume God gets angry. We treat people according to how they treat us; God must do the same.

When I was in high school, Jethro Tull came out with their hit album, *Aqualung*. The album's cover art had a picture of an ancient manuscript with the following words:

> In the beginning, Man created God
> In the image of Man created he him
> And Man gave unto God a multitude of names,
> That he might be Lord of all the earth . . .
> When it was suited to Man.

As a young, fervent Christian, I felt insulted by this idea. I was sure this was why youth ministers told us not to listen to rock and roll. The idea that man created God was deeply offensive to me.

However, as the years have progressed, and I have continued on the spiritual journey, as my images of God have come and gone, I've come to believe that Jethro Tull was right. We *often* create God in our own images.

That is not to say that it is good or bad that we do so, but simply to say that we do it. It is something our spiritual ancestors did. It is something we do today. We project onto God traits that are human. Of course we do. We can understand human, and we cannot understand the Divine.

It is okay that we do it. In fact, it is quite helpful for our spiritual lives. When I became a father, my experience of God was deepened by my visceral experience of parental love. Once I experienced fatherly love, I was able to project that experience onto the Divine. I learned experientially what people had been talking about when they said that God's love was deep and unconditional. Again, this was very helpful.

Some of the most beautiful and moving writing in history speaks of God in human terms. It is one of the best ways we make meaning. We compare something we *don't* know to something we *do*. We use what we *can* experience to understand and talk about that which we *cannot*.

So humanizing God is not a bad thing. It's just an incomplete thing.

So we do well when we acknowledge what we are doing. It is helpful when we are using images to talk about God to recognize that we are personifying that which cannot be contained. When we use language that cannot contain God, it is in our best interests to acknowledge that we are *not* describing God as God is.

An Enduring Metaphor: God as Person

In the quantum universe, a universe where illusion, uncertainty, and relativity have become the way things are, truths that are pinned down with certainty actually seem *less* true.

At the First Church Council of Nicea in 325 CE, the bishops all got together to figure out what we believed about God. Having experienced the Divine deeply in the care and nurture of creation and nature, we imagined God as a Father. Having also experienced the Divine deeply in both the person of Jesus and the indwelling presence of the Divine Spirit, we set out to articulate a way to talk about these dimensions of Divine experience. It was a bit of a pickle when we experienced God three ways and our Hebrew Scriptures insisted God was one, but we soldiered on.

After some head scratching, a great deal of consultation, and prayerful consideration, the bishops issued a proclamation about their deliberations. From then until now, the official church stance on the Christian God has been this: "Three Persons, One Substance."

"Three Persons, One Substance."

Once we began to talk about God that way, the idea of God as "person" became *the* normative image for our religion. Of all the ways we imagine God, this one is the one most likely to be confused for reality.

Our tradition contradicts itself on this point. On the one hand, we say that God is "person." On the other hand we say that God is "ineffable," uncontainable in any image, even the "person" image.

Once the Person-God became orthodoxy, we narrowed our collective imagination about God. The unintended consequence of framing God as a person (albeit a divine person), is that forever after, he will be a he, and he will have a mind like ours, feelings like ours, intent and purpose like we have. We have friends and enemies, likes and dislikes. God must, too.

And once that view of God gained historical momentum, other views seemed out of sync, seemed somehow off, and actually began to seem somewhat heretical. We began to protect our favored metaphor by rejecting others, and soon we had shoehorned God to fit in it. God was now person.

In this framework, our God is a being with human-like characteristics. It feels heretical to imagine God as an unseen force or power like electricity. The first *Star Wars* movies came out when I was a kid. The idea that "the Force might be with us," elicited more than a few hostile sermons. No! It cannot be! God is not a force. God is a person!

So there it is.

The appropriate and required metaphor for God: He is a he. He is a person.

The disallowed metaphor for God: anything else.

But if we want to be faithful to our Christian heritage, this is not our way.

We have always insisted on the humility of *not* defining the Ineffable, *not* standardizing spiritual experience into a single metaphor, *not* demanding everybody give allegiance to the one and only proper metaphor for God.

That is not our way.

It is not our way to shoehorn the deepest yearning of our hearts into a graven image. It is not our way to reduce our longing for the wild and unknowable Divine to a construct that fits in our heads. It is not our way to domesticate the Divine, or put it into a box of our own making.

To be sure, we do it. But how many of us share my daughter's anxiety, and have no alternative but the Father image of God?

It is the Christian way to move nimbly from God-metaphor to God-metaphor, extracting a wide and diverse experience of the Divine as we do.

5

Trade Your God In For a New One

My Son: A Story

As my son Michael and his friends were entering their driving years, tragedy struck. His best friend since second grade lost his sister to a terrible automobile accident. As you can imagine, my son's life was upended by the heartbreak. He struggled to be a comfort to his good friend, while at the same time coping with his own unraveling world. Disoriented, he had a chat with the youth minister of his friend's church. Well intentioned, this young minister spoke to him of God's higher purpose that we cannot understand. He talked about how love for God demands human beings have free choice, and how that choice always creates heartache and sorrow.

Michael has an affable personality. I rarely see him angry. But after that chat, he was livid.

Clearly, the tidy Christian narrative the minister had given him hadn't touched his hurt. When I suggested we get coffee and have a chat, he had a few choice words for me and all my Christian $#!&. "Don't even bother trying to tell me how God makes this kind of thing all right," he said. "There is nothing you can say to make this all right."

But he agreed to coffee.

We ordered. He vented. And after a while, he looked at me, my cue to begin.

"Michael, it's even worse than you know. You live in the safest, most comfortable part of the world. Losing a friend is horrible, horrible, horrible, but in other parts of the world, it often gets even worse. Boys younger than you are forced at gunpoint to kill their own families. The intent is to push them into doing something so terrible they can never return home. They want the boys to have no choice but to remain and fight for the army that captured them. Young girls, younger than you, are raped and impregnated as a matter of social policy. By forcing one group to bear the children of another, the conquering army can eliminate the ethnic bloodline they are trying to defeat.

"It can be horrible out there, Michael. The idea that there is a Supreme and Benevolent Being up there in heaven overseeing all this horribleness gets harder and harder to swallow.

"I can't swallow it anymore."

I think it surprised him that his father, the minister, said that out loud. I went on to tell him about losing my faith during my seminary years. I told him about some of the global and personal tragedies that had unraveled my own belief in a supreme, benevolent, Being-God. I told him about my own visceral reaction that had been very similar to his.

We spoke about how this painful unraveling process is actually an inevitable part of the spiritual journey. As we come to see the true terribleness in the world, it becomes increasingly difficult to hold on to the *Good-God-in-the-Sky* many of us grow up with.

"However," I suggested, "This unraveling process need not be the end of your religion. In fact, for many who have gone before you, it has actually been the gateway into a deeper and more powerful spiritual life. But, be prepared," I said. "If you follow this ancient and well-worn spiritual path, you won't come out with the same God you started with."

We spoke of a Christian faith rooted in experience rather than doctrine. I told him about the further reaches of the spiritual journey, where the *experience* of Divine Life and Divine Love trump doctrine and creedal belief. I told him the story of my own painful experience of unraveling belief, and how I subsequently awakened to the experience of Divine Life.

After we had chatted about a broader understanding of the spiritual journey, I told him that one of the byproducts of our transition from the religion of belief to the religion of experience is the need for new ways to think about

God. As we cast about for ways to talk about that which cannot be talked about, we have to try out new metaphors, new images.

I described for him one of the images that has become helpful to me, the image of God as Song.

"Instead of thinking of God as a guy up in heaven," I suggested, "imagine God as a Song that plays throughout the whole universe. This God-Song plays in your heart, in mine, at school, in our families, our jobs, our world, everywhere. Imagine this Song's powerful downbeat. It is the downbeat of love, joy, peace, patience, and kindness (the Fruit of the Spirit).[1] It is the downbeat of honesty, wisdom, prudence, courage, and so forth (the heavenly virtues). It is the downbeat of the things we experience when we experience God.

"And if we imagine God as a Song," I said, "it changes the expectations we bring to the spiritual journey. When God is a Supreme Being out there in heaven, we expect him to do this or do that. We ask ourselves why he would let this or that happen, why he wouldn't stop it.

"But when we think of God as a Song, it changes what we look for.

"If God is a Song, our central question stops being 'why.' It starts being whether or not we will dance.

"Whether a dear friend lives or dies, we must always decide if we will dance to the rhythm of love. When we experience tragedy or triumph, we are always deciding if we will dance the steps of kindness and goodness. In good times or bad, we are always choosing whether we will stand by the wall, or get out there on the floor and go for it.

"When the question changes, it changes in good times and bad. When our hearts are breaking or are overjoyed, we are always deciding if we will dance to the Song. We are always choosing if we will listen for the rhythm of the inner Presence, if we will respond as it draws us to move. The Song of divine courage is always playing, as is the Song of patience, wisdom, peacefulness, and compassion."

We can always dance to the God-Song, even when tragedy breaks our hearts.

Different ways of thinking about God evoke different questions about life.

1. Gal 5:22.

Different ways of thinking about God invite us to follow different spiritual journeys.

Different ways of thinking about God call us to different life experiences.

Trade Your God in for a New One

My twelve step friends tell me of a pithy saying they use. "When your God stops working for you, trade him in and get a new one."

That sounds offensive to many Christians, but I like it. It resonates with our heritage of humility. When the third of the twelve steps teaches us to turn our lives over to God as we understand God, it reminds us that we never understand God in any permanent way. We turn our lives over to God as we understand God *today*. But as we grow and are redeemed, we change. From our new vantage point, we see more clearly. We see what we could not see before. And from this new vantage point, we are able to see new dimensions of God, new facets of the Divine.

It is a necessary part of the spiritual journey, then, to trade in older understandings of God so we can embrace new ones.

As we saw in the last chapter, our tradition gives us permission for this trade-in practice. We've been doing it for years.

Our images of God continually evolve. After Jesus, Christians traded in the Hebrew God of reward and punishment for a new one. Jesus traded in the standard-setting God before whom we earned either favor or reprimand. He spoke of a God who gave rain and sun to bless just and unjust people alike.[2] He taught us a deeper version of God, a dimension of unconditional love. The early Christians updated God and our spiritual life so that "deserving" or "earning" became irrelevant. Grace became the centerpiece of our faith as we began to realize the depths of God's compassion and loving-kindness.

Each evolving image of God transforms the way we live. When God is a rewarder of good behavior and a punisher of bad, we do good deeds to avoid negative consequences. Our God determines the instincts we bring to our daily lives. Punishing gods make it more likely that we will punish one another, and create a *quid-pro-quo* world. If you do justly by me, I'll do justly by you. Wrong me, however, and like my God, I'll punish you.

2. Matt 5:45.

As we move beyond the reward-punish version of God it changes the way we relate to others. Instead of relating on the basis of what each deserves, we create a world in which we *are* our brother's keepers. If God cares for just and unjust alike, so can we. It is a truism that people become like the God they worship. When our God is merciful, we become merciful. When our God loves flawed people, we are more likely to look beyond one another's weaknesses.

Two Traditions: Apophatic and Kataphatic

Our contemplative ancestors taught us to live and thrive when our God is unknown and unknowable. Theirs was the wisdom that God's primary language is silence, and that we discover a vibrant faith soaking in the silence of meditation and contemplation. They introduced us to the spirituality of a God beyond images and metaphors. We use the word "apophatic" to describe this part of our spiritual tradition. Through the centuries, we've developed contemplative practices that awaken us to the Divine Presence beyond our mind's ability to contain.

The pursuit of God *with* thoughts, words, and emotions is also a rich part of our tradition. "Kataphatic" is the word we use to describe this spirituality. The doctrine of God's transcendence (unknowability) is not our only doctrine. We also have the doctrine of God's immanence. It tells us that in an imperfect and incomplete way, we *can* experience the Divine with our minds and our hearts.

However, since the Enlightenment, Western Christian spirituality has been almost exclusively kataphatic. We have tended to formulate images of God in our minds, and then configure our spiritual lives around them. As we've seen, even though these images move us deeply, over time we've tended to formalize them. We've tended to turn them into more than metaphors, more than images. We've often mistaken the metaphor for the reality. We do this unconsciously, not really noticing that we've reduced God to an image that fits in our minds. This shrinks our God, reduces our spirituality, and eventually stops working for us.

When this happens, we haven't always been very good about feeling our permission to trade in our old versions of God.

Julian of Norwich

Julian of Norwich is one of our church's saints. She lived in the fourteenth and fifteenth centuries and when she was thirty years old, a severe illness put her on her deathbed. There, she had a series of visions of Christ. She recovered, immediately recorded her visions, and survived into her 70s. She lived out her days as an anchoress in a small cell attached to the church of Norwich, England, and became one of our faith's best known contemplatives. Twenty years passed between the time of her illness and the days when she later rewrote her accounts of her visions with commentary born of her years of spiritual experience.[3]

One of the main themes of her life was to tinker with metaphors for God. As we saw earlier, the church given us by the Roman Empire loved uniformity. It is no surprise that they pushed for a standardized view of God. Julian, on the other hand, insisted that God could not be known that way, and that an appreciation of mystery was central to our experience of God.

God is our Mother, she said, as truly as God is our Father. We come from the Womb of the Eternal, she said. We are not simply made *by* God, we are made *of* God.[4]

Also, not willing to reduce God to a person metaphor, she insisted God is energy just as truly as God is being. We are not only made *by* God, we are made *of* God, containing within our own beings the animating energy of the Divine. If God is the very source of our being, it is by looking within ourselves that we find God, the very essence of our truest selves.[5]

God is in everything. God is nature's substance. Julian speaks of "smelling" God, "swallowing God in the waters and juices of the earth," and "feeling God in our bodies, in the body of all creation."[6]

In our contemplative tradition, God is not a presence that is separate from us but rather the energizing Reality that *makes us* humanity. God is the presence of love at the heart of creation, and the presence of life at the center of human beings, in the heart of all matter in the universe.

---

3. Julian, "*Revelations.*"

4. Julian, "*Revelations,*" para. 2.

5. Newell, *Christ of the Celts.* 468.

6. Ibid., 468.

The deeper we move into the human soul, the closer we come to the Divine. The nearer we are to our true selves, the more we sing the song of Divine Love.

You can't help but notice how Julian's and the contemplative view of God differ from the standard person metaphor.

When life insists it is time to trade in our old God for a new one, our saints, our contemplatives, and our tradition give us both permission and path.

Different Metaphors; Different Journeys

Imagining God differently, we experience the spiritual journey differently. That's the way it goes. When we imagine God as a person, we search for God within person-like parameters. God is a guy with friends, so we wonder if *we* are his friends. Many Christians live their lives in this insecurity, wondering if they've done enough to gain God's favor. Many of us labor away, either trying hard to please God, or we give up in despair, believing we just can't measure up. "Persons" have preferences. It is only natural to wonder if God prefers us.

When we imagine God as a man with a plan, and things go badly in our lives, we naturally assume we somehow misbehaved, somehow missed the plan, or somehow stepped out of God's will. Persons have plans, and if someone crosses their plans, they react badly. When something bad happens, we can't help but ask ourselves, "How did I upset the man with the plan?"

However, when we tinker with our God metaphors, perhaps think of God as Soil, Energy, or Song, we can deepen our spiritual lives. Updating our images of God changes our religion. When they pinch, our religion gives us permission to reimagine them, and we should.

God Is Love

Whenever we deepen our quest for God, love is what we find.

Though our tradition insists we cannot contain God in our minds, it also insists we can *experience* God. And when we do, we experience love. As we come to depend less and less on transient and impermanent images, our religion insists that the essential experience of God is of goodness and love. God is good. We are safe.

As our apophatic tradition leads us beyond images, we become more comfortable in the presence of divine mystery, not needing to frame a God who is "like this," or who will "do that." Instead, our contemplative practice awakens and feeds our ceaseless yearning for the Ultimate, for the Deep from which we come. Apophatic spirituality invites us to feel comfortable being one with divine Presence through inner quiet that does not try to direct or maneuver God.

The testimony of those who have gone before us is unanimous. When we focus on simply being present to the indwelling Presence, something happens to us. Our thoughts, feelings, and assumptions about God change. People of steadfast contemplative practice begin to frame God less as the metaphor-God, and more as an experience of love.

Whatever God is, we experience *his* nature, or *her* nature, or *its* nature (we struggle for language, don't we?) when we live in the experience of love.

This theme is repeated throughout the scriptures. Both kataphatic and apophatic spirituality affirm it. God is love. God is love. God is love. This ultimate Reality extends wherever we are, wherever we go. Divine Love-Nature is shot through everyone and everything: you, me, rocks and trees, sinners and saints. It is accessible to Christians and Jews, Hindus and Buddhists, Americans and Iraqis, everyone everywhere.

The experience of overarching Love is the point of walking the path of God. It is the quest for ultimate Reality. It is the quest for that which passes understanding.

A God of Love; A Life of Justice

As the experience of Divine Love deepens in us, we change. As we become increasingly present to the incomprehensible God, the expansiveness of Divine Love captures us. Taken on this spiritual journey we find ourselves unable to maintain the narrow focus of "me and mine," "how I feel," or "what I want." Those captured by the love of God inevitably focus on social justice. They invariably begin to care for the earth and its inhabitants.

One of Martin Luther King's most oft-quoted passages was Amos 5. He tended to use the poetic language of the King James Bible, but listen to that same passage in the gritty language of the street. Speaking for God, Amos says this:

> Quit with the burnt offerings already!
> Quit with the grain offerings!
> Quit with all the things you do to satisfy your religious requirements.
> You bring all the right stuff to me; you meet all your obligations . . .
> But stop! Go away! Quit bringing me these things.
> I have no regard for them.
> Don't sing me any more of your noisy songs.
> Don't play me any more of your pretty tunes.
> *Instead, go out and let justice run down like waters.*
> *Go out, and let righteousness flow like a mighty stream.*[7]

That is what Love does. That is what happens to those whose perspective of God steps back from any given metaphor, and becomes enveloped in our Love God.

At times in our religion we've really gotten this. Ours is a heritage rich with people who have fought for justice and rightness and goodness. Ours is a heritage rich with people who have sensed the divine impulse to care for the poor, the sick, and the imprisoned.

But at other times, ours has been a tradition focused on spiritual technologies designed to get God working for us. Our metaphor approach to God is often a thinly veiled attempt to direct or control God. We try to work the system so God will protect us from life's dangers and be our ally. We work hard so God will keep us safe and make us prosper. Through our prayers, behaviors, and rituals, we are in fact working to keep the Person-God working on our behalf.

At other times, ours has also been a heritage of immobilizing fear. We worry we may have earned the wrath or rejection of the Almighty Metaphor-God. We fear we will be severely punished for our failures or rejected for our sin. Many cringe in fear that the King-God, or Judge-God, or Father-God is displeased with them, or has formed a negative opinion of them. Thus absorbed, there is precious little bandwidth left over for social justice.

---

7. Amos 5:21–24 (personal paraphrase).

In the quantum era, a relative universe has produced a pluralistic society. In this social environment, the value of our religion will always be measured by how well we do in service to others.

Better images of God can help us. Deeper experiences of Love can help us.

If we want better instincts, if we want to become Christians who better the earth, if we want to do more than just better ourselves, we need new images of God. We need to transcend our reactionary fear of divine punishment. We need a deepened experience of Divine Love.

When our God no longer works for us. It's time to trade him in for a new one.

Jesus gave us a simple litmus test for measuring the worth of any construct. What kind of fruit does it bear?[8] A quick look at the condition of the church today indicates that our images of God are bearing bad fruit. We have the tradition. We have the permission. We ought to trade our tired images in for better ones.

8. Matt 7:16.

Rethinking Human Nature

6

Original Sin. Really?

James the Landscaper

James was a newcomer to our community and in a tough place when he came to talk with me. His financial situation had become dire. He was losing his house to foreclosure. Coming home to the power being shut off was commonplace. He wasn't meeting his family's needs, his kids were worried, and he was awake many nights in a panic over his situation.

When we met, I asked him how he had gotten to this place. He'd been a foreman with one of the larger landscaping companies in town, making a good living, running several crews. When he called the management on some financial shenanigans, he lost his job. Unable to find another one, he started his own company.

He began to target small clients, and charged well under market value to build a clientele. He landed several accounts, but over time, found himself unable to raise his prices without losing them.

As we spoke, I asked about his service. "Better than most," he said. I asked about his salesmanship. This was also better than most. Then I asked him why he targeted clients who couldn't pay the going rate. He scratched his chin for a moment, and then admitted he didn't think clients willing to pay top dollar would choose him over his competitors. I asked if his service was as good as theirs, and he admitted that it was.

"Why wouldn't they choose you, then?" I asked.

After a while, our conversation became less about business and more about James's interior world. He struggled with insecure feelings when he was around established businesses or clients who could pay. Consequently, he said, he'd been focusing his energies on clients who couldn't really afford him.

"Why do you feel insecure about your business, when it's as good or better than your competitors?"

After some more conversation, he began to talk about his ongoing battle with his doubt about the worth and value he brought to the table. As often happens, our conversation turned to rejections and hurts from his past.

All stories eventually track back to the story we believe we are living, so I began to ask him about his view of God, his view of himself, and his view of human nature in general.

As we continued, it became clear that he'd grown up with a heavy dose of sin consciousness. In his religion, God was displeased with people, always mildly angry at them for being so consistently sinful. His belief was reinforced by his interpretation of the hard times he was in. He saw them as divine punishment for past failures. Instead of a story that helped him rise above his negative experiences, his told him that this was his lot in life, that he shouldn't really expect anything more. In his story, human beings are "totally depraved," "originally sinful," and hopelessly infected by the death nature of sin. Consequently, God, the embodiment of holiness, could not abide to be in the presence of sinful creatures such as ourselves.

If we dig deeply enough, most problems eventually become theological problems.

For James, the problems of a failing business were rooted in personal insecurities, which were in turn rooted in a series of negative personal experiences. How he had interpreted and integrated those experiences into his life was determined by the story he was told about the way things are.

And James is not alone. Many faithful Christians have been told a story in which their essential nature is foul and corrupt.

We can do better.

Embracing Paradox

Before we can talk about human nature, we have to talk about paradox. People are nothing if not paradoxical.

In the last five hundred years, ambiguity has fallen on hard times. As we've seen, Enlightenment era folks prefer their truth precise and unwavering. The ability to hold two seemingly disparate truths in our minds at one time has atrophied over these last centuries. Truths with two sides to them are uncomfortable in a precise, mechanical, and certain universe. Not until our physics changed did it become necessary to once again experience our great truths in tension with other seemingly incongruent ones.

As we've seen, this shouldn't be a problem for Christians. Our most cherished truths come to us this way. God is one; God is three. Jesus is human; Jesus is divine. God is just; God is merciful.

Though paradox is embedded in our doctrines, for the last few centuries our minds haven't been open to explore truth this way. We gave assent to our ancient binary truths because they were part of our tradition, but our brains were wedded to a precise worldview. Paradox just created internal dissonance. To cope, we tended to simply drop one of the truths held in tension. For many generations now, it has been our practice to quietly choose one truth in a paradoxical couplet, pay attention to it, and ignore the other. We saw earlier how we did this with our dual doctrines about scripture. Our tradition teaches us that the Bible is the word of God *and* the words of men. However, we have tended to embrace the former and ignore the latter.

We can be excused for our discomfort. It's just not the way the Enlightenment universe worked. However, our universe has changed, and if we want to do a better job telling the Christian story, it is now necessary to return to our ancient ways and reacquaint ourselves with the paradoxical nature of truth.

This is especially true when we come to telling the story of human nature. Our scriptures tell us that we are of two natures, made in the image of God— and at the same time, carrying the nature of sin. As could have been expected, we've tended to focus on one and ignore the other. At least since the time of the Reformers, ours has been a singular focus on the sinful nature of humanity.

The Human Self: Made of the Same Stuff God Is

Listen to these paraphrased words from the first pages of the Bible:

> God created human beings.
> He created them godlike, reflecting his own nature.
> God looked over everything he had made . . .
> And it was good, so very good![1]

With those few words, our tradition laid out a radical conception of human nature. "Created in the very image and likeness of God," that's how we say it today. "*Imago Dei*," that's how we used to say it when we still spoke Latin.

In our story, humans first show up in a garden where we are being formed out of dirt and animated by God's very breath. Divine presence fills and awakens us. This fundamental narrative, given us from the beginning, tells us who we are. We are made of stardust (dirt) and we are made of God-dust (the breath of God). We are fashioned of earth, and we are made alive by the breath of the Divine. We may hide our divine nature well, but it *is* our intrinsic nature. Divinity is woven into our very beings, inextricably bound up within us.

The image of God is not a character trait we put on or take off. It's not like being kind or unkind, one day one, the next day the other. No! The divine image is *the* essential ingredient of being human.

Neither is the divine image an attribute we take on when we are baptized as Christians. It is, our story tells us, the very essence of our humanity. Before there was a Christian story to tell, the divine image was already vested in the very center of the human soul. We are sacred, not because we have prayed the sinner's prayer or because we have been baptized. There are good reasons for these practices, but they do not make us sacred. We are sacred simply because we exist, simply because we were created.

Consequently, when we touch our truest selves, we touch the Divine. There is wisdom within us, greater than the foolishness in which we so often live. There is a virtue within us, greater than the vice we so often commit. There is kindness within us, greater than the meanness we so often express. But most of all, deep within us there is unbounded love. These attributes exist at the center of every human being because every human being is made in the

---

1. Gen 1:26-31 (excerpts).

image of God. This essential ingredient of our nature is a deeper and truer and more real part of us than any lesser nature that infects our souls after the fact.

We can't tell a better Christian story unless we return to this ancient starting point.

In a healthy story, *imago Dei* must inform our essential instincts about ourselves and one another. It must inform how we interpret weakness, failure, and sin. If the divine is our truest essence, then we are not *defined* by weakness or failure. Of course, if divinity is our truest essence, neither are we defined by our successes or victories. Sin and shame do not define us. Nor do we need to drive ourselves to earn worth or value. Simply by virtue of our existence, we are breathtakingly precious, extraordinarily magnificent, and essentially made of the same stuff God is made of.

The Human Self: Carrying a Dark Side

But being made of the same stuff God is made of—that's not the whole story, is it?

It is a universally recognized human experience that there are two natures within us. We see in ourselves the noble and the divine; we see virtue, graciousness, and decency. But we also carry within ourselves the ignoble, the base, the scandalous, the unethical, and the indecent.

Trying to explain and deal with these competing natures has been the jurisdiction of religion from the beginning. In the traditional telling of the Christian story, we talk about "the fall," or "sin nature," to explain this second, dark, scandalous side of our humanity. We have been captured by a lesser, more base version of ourselves that acts as a mask, a guise over our true selves. Theologians and spiritual teachers call this dark persona that is separate from our true, divine centers the "false self."

When we live as more base versions of ourselves, we fall into a lower state of existence. Ours have become lives of falseness and ignorance. It is as though we can no longer remember our true beings, our true beginnings, and we are living in a deep sleep, under the sway of a counterfeit nature, a counterfeit identity.

Some part of us knows we are not living our truest selves, and our disconnectedness from our own nature drives us into a deep and abiding anxiety. This, in turn, drives us to words, deeds, motivations, and actions that create broken lives and a broken world. We become slaves to falseness, condemned to lives of anxiety and vice.

But note what we are *not* saying. We are not saying that our essential divine nature has somehow disappeared or been fundamentally altered. Instead, we're saying that our human race has become disconnected from our true, divine centers. A sinful nature has become an overlay on our true centers, a veneer that profoundly and negatively impacts our lives, but never removes or replaces our truest nature.

You Are Not Your Sin

Growing up as a kid in church, my ministers often used the metaphor of physical illness to talk about our lower natures. We've been infected by the sin virus, they said. Now that I'm older and have had some time to reflect on that way of thinking, this image makes even more sense. When our bodies get sick, it's awful, but even so, we don't think our ailing bodies define us. Illness doesn't define us, it just infects us. Likewise, a sinful nature does not define us, it just infects us.

One of our spiritual ancestors, Eriugena, an Irish philosopher, scholar, and theologian from the ninth century, called sin "leprosy of the soul."[2] Leprosy distorts the body and makes us appear monstrous. Sin does the same. In fact, it can so distort us that we come to believe the disease of sin to be the face of the human soul. Just as leprosy deadens sensation, sin deadens our sensitivity to that which is deepest in us, truest about us. We come to believe, act, and live as though we are *not* made in the image of God. But it is no more true that leprosy defines the ill person than it is that sin defines the sinful person. Sin is an overlay, an infection, not an identity.

Not Our Truest Selves; But No Small Thing

Saying that sin does not define our truest human nature is not to say that it is a trifling. Not at all. The ancients, who understood our nature so well,

2. Leaver, "*Celtic*," para. 103.

teach us that sin is a formidable foe. Theirs was not the view that our true selves could be easily recovered. A sinful nature might be a veneer, but it is not a thin one.

The infection of the human soul is serious and unrelenting. Greed, lust, pride, envy, wrath, and all manner of vice infect us deeply. They are cancerous adversaries, and their removal is a daunting undertaking. Eriugena compared sin to a lion, pouncing on everything that is born. It is always lurking at the door. It hovers, he says, at the door of the womb, ready to infect everything that comes into being.[3]

But as formidable a foe as sin is, we cannot mistake it for the self. This fundamental misconception has negatively impacted the spiritual journeys of many Christians, today and through the centuries. We mistakenly define the spiritual life as a battle with sin, making it the centerpiece of our story, giving it far too much power and attention.

Once we define the spiritual journey as a battle with sin, we *don't* focus on returning to our true selves.

A sin-focused story misses the point. It makes us think about human nature selectively. We heed carefully those scriptures that speak of sin and shortcomings, but ignore those that tell us our nature is fundamentally of God. We see ourselves behaving badly: thinking, feeling, and acting in ways that are hurtful, and we believe *this* is the truest part of ourselves.

To live this debased version of life, we have to overlook, or at least deemphasize, our *image of God* doctrine. We forget that our story goes deeper than sin, telling us we are created *by* God and *of* God. We downplay our story's fundamental truth, that we are alive because the indwelling presence of God has been breathed into us.

When we restore balance to our self-perception, it fundamentally changes the Christian story we live.

Original Sin, Total Depravity, and Punitive Spirituality

The Christian doctrine of *original sin* and its harsher cousin, *total depravity*, have had a lot to do with our selective way of seeing our own natures. These

3. Newell, *Christ*, 5.

doctrines helped explain the ugly, hurtful, wounded, and wounding parts of us. They told us there is a real, present, and powerful dark side in all of us. If that's all the doctrines did, they could be helpful when thinking and talking about the human condition.

It's quite possible the doctrines of original sin and total depravity began this way, as simple descriptors of the darkness inside us. However, the word "sin" has come to mean something else as the years have gone by. In current usage it is a synonym for "culpability" or "crime." Today, the word "sin" means the evil we do, say, or think. When we add the adjective "original" in front of the idea of criminal deeds, we come to think of the doctrine like this: "I'm very, very bad. I know so, because of all the bad things I do. I do them even when I try not to. It must be that my very nature is bad, and thus, I am bad.

"And look at you! You're just as bad as I am. You hurt me. You perpetrate wars. Your Wall Street greed hurts me. You rape. You murder. It must be," we conclude, "that we're *all* bad. We were probably born bad and never had a chance! Humans must just inherit wicked genes, making our nature fundamentally bad."

This common Christian narrative isn't an unreasonable conclusion. Look around.

During the Reformation, Calvin added in *total depravity* for emphasis. The essence of human nature, he said, is totally evil, totally corrupt, totally perverse, and totally reprobate. Apart from a metamorphic transformation by God, the Reformers concluded, human nature is intrinsically bereft of any redeeming quality.

Gone was any hint of *imago Dei*.

Over the years, our story has been told almost exclusively in terms of fundamental corruption and perversion. When these doctrines are the building blocks of the story we tell ourselves, it erodes our collective sense of self. If our religion tells us horrible things about our basic nature for enough generations, it tends to give us a collective sense of self-hatred and blinds us to the glorious divinity within.

Some Christians take a notoriously harsh posture toward themselves. Others mitigate things with ideas about a loving God. Either way, when we believe we are fundamentally evil, our spiritual instincts are to keep our corrupt nature on a tight leash. Our spiritual instincts tend toward the brutal. We no longer beat ourselves with whips as we did in previous generations, but we still beat ourselves up. To keep what we believe is our true nature under control, we impose on ourselves harsh guilt and self-condemnation. We make our failures costly affairs in the belief that by doing so, we'll be less inclined to repeat them in the future. Ours becomes a self-punishing form of spirituality. By force of punishment, we try to corral our sinful nature, and pummel it into submission.

And the thing is, this punitive approach works for a while. It really does help us modify our behaviors. With a great deal of effort, many have been able to alter negative habits, often for extended periods of time. However, this approach carries with it some really awful side effects.

When our approach to ourselves is a punitive one, it isn't long before we begin to feel and act punitively toward one another. Ours becomes a brittle and dogmatic intolerance of one another's failures. A sin-centric religion, a sin-centric spirituality, makes our focus the battle with our own sin, but extends to battling one another's sin.

I first started hearing the term "religious abuse" or "church abuse" when I was a young minister. Church folks began to notice authoritarian leaders increasingly positioned to control or dominate parishioners. Scolding, rebuking, chastening, and even ostracizing had become commonplace means of controlling people. Often spiritual leaders were positioned above their community, above accountability. Theirs became the role of defining sin and failure, pointing it out, and levying the reprimands and rebukes necessary to straighten people out.

More than a few good people have left their Christian communities reeling from the pain and damage sustained at the hands of unwise, abusive, authoritarian spiritual leaders.

I know some of those leaders. For the most part, they are not control freaks or power-hungry monsters. Few people become ministers because they want to dominate others. No, these are sincere, well-intentioned, earnest people who are trying their best to serve God and their communities.

Their problem is their story.

Believing people are totally depraved by their infection with original sin, what else is a sincere minister to do, but try his or her best to keep folks from falling into the abyss of their flawed natures?

The reasoning seems sound, but *this* story bears the fruit of harshness, rigidity, intolerance, fear, and a well behaved, but battered community of faith.

Again, the litmus test Jesus gives us for judging the truthfulness of an idea is the fruit it bears. Simply looking around suggests that this way of thinking about original sin could use some reconsidering.

A Self-Fulfilling Doctrine

When we believe the total-depravity version of our story, it has a self-fulfilling effect upon us.

If you're listening to the world, you know our Christian reputation has been terribly sullied. And for good reason. Many of the things we say out loud are awful! People see us as intolerant, judgmental, narrow-minded, self-absorbed, and hypocritical. Those are pretty good synonyms for what we say about ourselves, "totally depraved." The troubling thing is that the story we tell ourselves has had a causal effect in making us this way.

When we believe our sin is original and our very essence depraved, our only hope is to be magically changed. We see salvation in Jesus as the way that change happens. Our salvation has to fundamentally alter our nature, making us new creatures, finally acceptable to God. Jesus doesn't save us by awakening us to our always-present interior divine image. No, that self is gone and our only hope is a new self.

There's a troubling implication when we tell our story this way. If our fundamental essence must be changed to be with God, then once it happens, once we pray the prayer, or get baptized, or do whatever we do to get "saved," we become essentially different from, alien to, the rest of humanity. They, having not had this essence-altering spiritual experience, are different from us.

This puts us directly at odds with the rest of the human beings on the planet. We are "us," and they have to be "them." We're not, after all, even the same kind of beings. They're mere humans. We're "new creatures." Difference and discord is sown between us at the level of defining essence. We are not in the same world they are, not living the same lives they are, not subject to the same nature they are. We are separate, set apart, a peculiar people, a holy people. They, on the other hand, are unregenerate, totally depraved heathens.

This changes us. And not for the better. No wonder the world is rejecting our story. It is a little disingenuous to call such a message "the gospel," the "good news."

Rethinking Original Sin

But we don't have to frame our doctrine of original sin this way. We could think of it very differently.

Instead of seeing it as a way to talk about universal *culpability*, we could use it to talk about a universal *wound*. We could use it to describe our universal human sense of dislocation from our true, divine-image selves.

Seeing sin as a wound rather than a nature elicits a kindhearted, magnanimous response. We are patient with ourselves when we are wounded. Also, we are empathetic toward others who have been wounded. Injury evokes empathy. It evokes the instinct to help. When we see this way, we recognize that unacceptable behavior is a result of the wound, not the self. We can be much more patient with people whose wound has disoriented them.

When our story speaks of a universal soul wound, we are less scandalized when darkness shows up in our lives, or in one another. It is to be expected. Knowing we all carry the hurt, our instinct is to share it together, to act compassionately toward ourselves and one another.

Rethinking universal sin breeds camaraderie among Christians, and between Christians and the rest of humanity. When our sin is a wound rather than a nature, we seek healing instead of a magically altered version of self. When sin is amnesia, we try to remember who we truly are instead of condemning ourselves for who we believe ourselves to be. Telling the story of our sin this way, we are able to jettison the condemnation and self-hatred so many Christians carry. Instead, we set out on a quest together, to find our way back to our true natures, our true selves, looking to Jesus to point the way.

Forewarned by our doctrine, we are forearmed to deal with the two selves we find within us. Forewarned, we seek out the Spirit's aid to find and return to our divine-image selves, our true centers. Forewarned, we join one another on a common quest to overcome our wound, heal from our disease, and move past the veneer. Seeing ourselves now and forever as one with God, our common quest is to return to our truest selves and deepen our experience of divine union.

Rethinking our doctrine of original sin deepens our spiritual lives, awakens us to the *imago Dei* within us, orients us to the quest before us, and makes allies instead of adversaries with our co-travelers on this journey.

7

Leftovers from Gnostic Dualism

Plato and a Two-Dimensioned Reality

We Christians think our views about things come from the Bible, or from God, or even from our own Christian ancestors, but this is not always so. Our view of human nature, for example, has been more influenced by the Greek philosopher Plato than by Jesus. About four hundred years before Jesus, Plato laid out a framework for thinking about reality that sits at the foundation of the way Western Christians think and feel about their nature.

In his parable, *The Cave*, Plato suggested that humans are like a man chained from birth to a chair at the back of a cave. Behind him, out of sight, is a fire he cannot see. In front of the fire are puppeteers operating marionettes and casting shadows on the wall before him. The shadows are the only existence he has known, so he comes to think of them as reality, as the way things are.

For us, Plato contended, the world we know—the world of objects, people, time, and place—is the shadow world. It is not reality. The real world, he taught us, exists somewhere else, somewhere outside this shadow land of our current experience. *That* world contains reality as reality truly is. *That* world contains the abstract ideal of all things in a perfect form. It is from this abstract ideal form that our physical world derives its reduced, derivative, shadow existence. For example, I am sitting at a table as I write this sentence. In Plato's view, this table is a derivative reduction, a shadow of the pure concept of "table" that exists in its true form out there in the real realm. While I sit here, my wife passes by the door and winks at me on her way to the other room. I laugh and feel a sense of love for her. However, that love, Plato teaches us, is a reduced, derivative shadow of the perfect concept of love that exists out in that other realm. When an idea, an experience, or an object leaves its pure, abstract, non-physical existence in that other realm, and when it gets shoehorned into the physical world we live in, it is reduced, tainted, and made somehow lesser.

And this Greek view of reality, it turns out, has had a lot to do with the way Western Christians think about our own human nature.

As Christianity's center of gravity moved west over the two centuries after Jesus, it didn't just move geographically. It moved from one worldview to a profoundly different one. Our story, having been cast in terms comfortable to Middle Eastern Hebrews, had to be recast to fit into a Greek, Western worldview. The story of Christianity had to be rethought and retold so that it could fit into the Platonic idea of a greater and lesser reality (ours being the lesser).

At the same time Christianity was hammering out its foundational teachings, Plato was making a comeback in the Roman Empire. Neo-Platonic teachers were adopting his teachings, keeping them alive, and at the same time, the Gnostics were re-crafting Platonic thought into a religious form. Their religion agreed that reality is divided into a world of pure forms and a shadow world. The pure world was out there, and the derivative world was here, where we are.

Early Christians had to grapple with these ideas floating around the Empire, and went back and forth trying to figure out how much to cast our story in Neo-Platonic or Gnostic terms, and how much to resist those ideas. Some key bishops resisted the Platonic-Gnostic influence, but for all their resistance, many of the sensibilities of a dualistic reality crept into the Christian story.

You can feel the influence today. We Christians feel in our guts that reality exists in two dimensions. The most important dimension, the spiritual, heavenly dimension, exists in a non-material form "out there" somewhere. This dimension isn't accessible to our five human senses, but it does possess the highest, most fundamental essence of all things. Influenced by this worldview, Christians have tended through the centuries, to put God, spirit, *logos*, heaven, angels, truth, wisdom, and virtue in the perfection realm. Humans, on the other hand, live in the lesser world, the material world of earth; rocks and trees, men and women, bodies and babies, blood and bones. Unconsciously following Platonic instincts, we grant the material world diminished status. It is lesser. It is derivative, illusory, and temporary.

When the Gnostics were figuring out a religion to resonate with this two dimension worldview, they took it one step further than Plato. They added moral character to the two realms. They insisted that the non-material realm was morally good, while the physical world was morally bad. The physical world became the arena of evil and corruption.

Trying to fit our story into terms that worked for Western people was something of a challenge. Our Genesis account insisted that God had made all of creation, and had repeatedly pronounced it good. However, as Christianity migrated west, the idea that the world of land and sea, of bodies and babies, was intrinsically good became hard to intuit. The word "flesh" became synonymous with "evil." Our view of the material world began its descent from divine joy and intrinsic goodness to debased immorality and derivative degeneracy.

Human Nature Torn Between Two Realms

For much of our history, our Christian view of ourselves has been informed by the two dimension universe. We have thought of ourselves as containing, and being contained in, both of these realms. We have bodies (the material world), but we also have souls (the perfection realm). These two parts of our nature exist in binary opposition to one another, as spirit and flesh. We've been steeped in the idea that the human spirit is our pure nature, made good by its association with God and the spiritual world. Our human bodies on the other hand, are associated with the limited, reduced, immoral, physical, material dimension. Spirit is good. Flesh is at best limited and at worst, evil.

This idea is so rooted in our thinking that many Christians believe this is just the way things are. However, this is actually a quasi-Christian idea we picked up from a philosophy and a religion that were competing for mind space with Judeo-Christianity in the years immediately after the apostles. Platonism and Gnosticism have been traveling companions of Christian thought for centuries.

Early Christian councils agreed that the Platonic-Gnostic idea of dual realities directly contradicted the teachings of Jesus, Paul, and the disciples.

However, even though Gnosticism itself died out, it infected Western Christianity so thoroughly during those formative years, that vestiges remain alive even today. Like a flu virus, it periodically returns through the centuries, attacking our fundamental view of ourselves.

When the Gnostics shaped the two dimension idea into a religion, they told a story of human nature like this. Human beings are pure, good, divine souls, but we are trapped in evil, corrupt, fleshy bodies. When they encountered Christianity, they politely absorbed Jehovah into their pantheon of gods, but reduced him to lower status. The Judeo-Christian God, they conceded, created the cosmos, but that meant he must have been a lower god. The true godhead god would never meddle in something as corrupt as the material world. Their highest god, Pleroma, was a supremely transcendent deity who inhabited the dimension of abstract purity, spiritual purity, existing above the mundaneness of physical existence.

When these sensibilities began to mingle with the newly emerging Christian religion, they mounted a challenge to the Genesis account that the material world is essentially good. Jews and early Christians savored and loved the material world, seeing God's presence in physicality of all kinds. The new Gnostic-Christian mix, however, introduced the idea of spirit-matter dualism. Spirit came from Pleroma, but flesh came from the lesser Jehovah. Consequently, while the material world was a necessary evil, transient and temporary, the spiritual world was where real value could be found. The spirit world lasts forever, the spirit world is precious, the spirit world is real, and thus, the spirit world is to be pursued.

For Gnostic-infected Christianity, spirit became good, and matter became evil.

Dislocated from Our Bodies; from the Earth

Through the centuries, as Christians worked through these conflicted sensibilities, most of us came to see our own natures through neo-Platonic lenses. Even today we tend to think of our beings as a battleground, existing in the tension between spirit and flesh, between good and evil. When, in those first few centuries, our bodies became depraved, we responded by learning to suppress their baser urges. The love of food, the savoring of ice cream, these were a function of our lower nature and as such, were to be avoided. Sexual appetite was of the material world, thus an impediment to the spiritual path.

We began to see our spiritual disciplines through the "buffet-the-flesh" lens.[1] We fasted to suppress our delight with food. We practiced celibacy to suppress our sexual desires. We practiced vigils to suppress the physical desire for sleep, wore horsehair shirts to suppress the desire for comfort. We went barefoot to suppress the physical desire for warmth. At every turn, physical desire was seen as an obstacle to the spiritual path, so like other Mediterranean religions of the day, Christianity pursued spiritual maturity by putting down these desires.

And here we are today, still under the influence of this Gnostic-Platonic-Christian mix. Many of us have been taught explicitly or tacitly that sexual desire and pleasure are something to be ashamed of, that body desires are not to be trusted, that this material world will burn, and only the spiritual will survive.

This way of telling our story through the years has tended to dislocate us from the physical world, from the very world given us to inhabit. This version of our story dislocates us from our bodies and our environment.

By the fifth century, this Gnostic-Christian hybrid religion had taken such a powerful hold over Western Christianity that the story had to be modified to fit. Instead of the Christ child being conceived in Mary's womb, conception took place in her ear, by spoken word only.[2] These mental gymnastics would make us laugh if they hadn't done so much damage to so many in our faith. When we sever the spiritual from the physical, we deny the proclamation that begins our story: "It is good, it is good, it is so very good!"

In my own church upbringing, there was a tacit understanding that the best way to spend one's life was in ministry. Secular careers had to be tolerated as necessary evils, but they were really settling for second best. Designing circuits, plumbing houses, or making films were activities of the material world, not really spiritual endeavors. They were distractions. The joys that came from them, the joys accrued creating something here on earth, were not nearly as important as religious endeavors.

As we're rethinking our story for the quantum era, it is important to understand how our instincts have evolved, how our thoughts about material existence have been infected with ugliness and existential flaw. Demonizing

1. 1 Cor 9:27.
2. Schihl, "*Immaculate*," para. 4.

the natural parts of our being—food, sex, sleep, and comfort—we remove them from the sacred and set ourselves up for a kind of craziness. Notice the absurd relationship our society has with food and sex. We can lay the responsibility for that at the feet of the Greek influence of early Christianity. Alienated from our bodies, and from the very earth, we created a society of rejection and insecurity.

How Convenient for the Romans

The idea that spirit is good and flesh is bad worked well for the Roman Empire. Intent on conquering the known world, the doctrine of a distant Creator who disdained matter was very convenient. If you're going to crush human bodies, it's convenient to believe that they are not sacred. If you're going to dominate the land of other peoples, it is advantageous to believe that land itself is not sacred. If you're going to exploit Creation, it helps to believe it is rotten anyway.

And this was just as true of the Roman Empire under the Caesars as it was of the French empire under Charlemagne or the British Empire under Elizabeth I. It was true of the Nazis in the 1930s, and remains true of the American empire today.

When any group seeks to build an empire, the sacredness of matter, the sacredness of human bodies, and the sacredness of the material world get in the way. Sadly, as we've degraded the Genesis proclamation of the material world's intrinsic goodness, the church has often been a collaborator with empires, blessing domination, and accommodating exploitation. Though clearly not the teaching of Jesus, this way of seeing human nature has often made us complicit in the power shenanigans of empires. Despite our many shining moments, influenced by this dualistic view of human nature, our church also has many dark moments. In bed with empire builders, we've often given doctrinal approval to colonialism, imperialism, slavery, and all kinds of abusive practices that crush human bodies, destroy human communities, and exploit human lands.

Alienation

The word "alienation" is a key interpretive lens through which scholars analyze the twentieth century. In the study of history, philosophy, psychology, or sociology, whenever we look at Western thought or experience, that word keeps popping up.

How could it not? For centuries the church had great influence in the West. After all that time, in the last one hundred fifty years, our body-spirit dualism has begun to catch up with us. Twentieth century technology amplified our instincts, resulting in savage world wars, unrestrained colonial exploitation, and recurring genocide. Reflective Westerners can't help but be plagued by the instincts that drive these horrors. What's wrong with us? What's wrong with me? Why do our instincts drive us apart, separating and isolating us? Why are we so estranged from our world, our work, and our people? What's wrong with us?

Disconnected from ourselves, from one another, from society, and from the earth, we instinctively create economic, political, technological, and social structures infected with dislocation. When we stopped seeing the sacredness of the physical world we became increasingly disconnected from the experience of God in the earthiness of this world, in the fleshiness of our bodies, in mothers, fathers, sisters, and brothers. We lost the experience of the divine in our food, among the rocks, grasses, animals, and sky.

Devoid of the sacred in the material, life was reduced to a marketplace, and people to competitors. In the unsacred world, villages, clans, tribes, and neighborhoods became utilitarian tools to be discarded in service to individual competition for a larger piece of the unsacred pie. We divided from one another, no longer revering the mysterious and hallowed world we lived in together. Ours became instead, a dog-eat-dog world.

Matter never stopped being sacred; Western Christians just stopped seeing it that way. When we did, ours became a culture of estrangement, estranged from the earth, from one another, and from the spiritual that is present in the very earthiness of our bodies.

How could it not have been so? We live in bodies, physical bodies. How could the divine ever inhabit something so material? How could the Holy Spirit ever indwell such corrupted housing?

When our story alienates us from our own bodies and from our own planet, we reject an important part of the spiritual life. We stop trying to experience God in the material world and miss its daily display of the divine. We stop hearing the voice of God in the physical world; the world, after all, is mere refuse that will surely burn. We internalize the pithy sayings of our grandparents: "This world is not our home; we're just passing through." We feel like strangers, outsiders, resident aliens in a foreign land. Our true home is the place of pure spirit, far away from here, out there in heaven.

A Toxic Story

Thus influenced, our story comes out something like this:

> We were born into a beautiful garden as pure beings. Sadly, evil invaded our souls, and was so powerful that it changed the very nature of our humanity and fractured the intrinsic goodness of the universe. Human sin fundamentally altered the nature of the planet and physical matter became so infected that nothing other than depravity and debasement could be expected. The DNA of our souls and our planet was corrupted.
>
> Consequently, the future of this earth is total destruction. Different Christians have different versions of how and when that will happen, but inevitably, the only future for our planet is to burn. And when it does, Christian people will be whisked away to a place of pure spirit, free from the ravages of matter and the physical world.
>
> Our posture on the earth, then, is to be one of waiting patiently until we go to heaven where we'll find our heart's true home. We should not get too connected to this corrupted garden; these are temporary digs for us. We shouldn't unpack our bags. Ours is the role of an estranged alien and outsider.
>
> We do have a job to do while we're here; it is to preach the message that the garden will soon burn, and that only true followers of God will be taken away. Ours is to tell people to join us in committing their hearts to spirit God, and then begin waiting with us for destruction and our hasty get-away.

This is an awfully poisonous way to tell the Christian story, isn't it?

However, this *is* the story we get when our starting point is one of a pure spirit trapped in an evil body. With that belief about human nature, we can be nothing else but foreigners in a strange land awaiting our escape from a doomed universe. It is no wonder so many Christians have little concern for the planet. This version of our story gives very little incentive to repair the earth. Why would we? The earth is a sinking ship.

How unlike the teachings of Jesus.
How unlike our church in its finest hours.

A Better Story about Human Nature

Gnostic-Platonic dualism hasn't always had such influence on our story. Quite regularly we step away from that narrative and emphasize union with God as our deepest identity. When this is our story, we tend not to collaborate with empires. At these times, we stress that matter *does* matter, and that we must revere the physical world. At these times we teach one another to experience God's presence in the created world, and that the entire universe is alive with the movement of Spirit. At these times, we see that Christ doesn't lead us *away* from matter, but more deeply into a daily resonance with the Holy Spirit that is always present in and around us.

At these times, our sense of self is built on the truth that God made everything and pronounced it good. God put divinity into the material world and so everything is sacred. Sometimes we have taught one another the doctrine of *creatio ex nilo* (God made the universe of nothing), but at other times we've taught that God made the universe of God's very self, breathing Divine Life and Divine Word into everything. Thus, we've taught, the land is sacred, the animals are sacred, our bodies are sacred, and human societies are sacred. Everything is *by* God, *of* God, and pronounced good, so of course it is all sacred. At these times, it has been our expectation to experience the Divine in the material world, in nature, in human society, in art, literature, science, and politics.

St. Francis talked about communing with God in solidarity with the birds, the insects, the sun, and the moon. In his unified, harmonious version of Christianity, the *best* place to look for God was in the material world. At its best, our religion has taught us that we can sense the Divine in the food we eat, in the trees that give us air to breathe, in the bodies of our lovers, and in the smell of our children. The sacred is to be found in our senses, our muscles and ligaments, and our bones and blood. God inhabits those very material parts of our humanity.

God is as close as close can be, and can be experienced in our lungs, legs, and the dirt we walk on. Elizabeth Barrett Browning put it this way:

> Earth's crammed with heaven,
> and every common bush afire with God.
> Only he who sees, takes off his shoes.
> The rest sit round it and pluck blackberries.

This is our Christian story.

Sin did not erase the divine nature that defines us, but merely caused us to forget it. Sin caused us to become disconnected from our true selves, and to drift from the experience of our essential nature. Consequently, we're so confused, bewildered, and cast adrift that we're unable to recall who we truly are, unable live from our true centers.

In this confused state, we believe the lie that this lesser version of us is who we are.

The spiritual journey, then, becomes about finding our true selves rather than having our true selves fixed or altered. The spiritual life, the experience of "being saved," is about being restored to what already is, not about becoming something fundamentally different.

This may seem merely a semantic difference, a minor shift of perspective. However, at a visceral level, it profoundly affects the way we are Christian.

We are made *by* God and we are *of* God. We are sons and daughters of the Divine. The good news, the gospel, is that it is possible to be restored to our true and rightful place, to return to being one with, not fundamentally opposed to, the Source from which we come. We are intimately linked to God at our very cores and are, as Jesus prayed in John 17, in our essence, one with the transcendent Supreme.[3]

Yes, sin is also part of our nature. Yes, we have lost our sense of God and our sense of self along the way, but the gospel, the good news, was given to us to awaken us to our true and ultimate destiny.

The work of the Christian journey is the work of remembering, the work of awakening from slumber, and being found when we are lost. The Christian message points us back to who we truly are.

3. John 17:21.

As we'll see in subsequent chapters, this changes our understanding of the redemptive work of Christ. Instead of salvation changing our essential nature, we experience it awakening us from slumber and pointing us back to what has always been our destiny: extensions of divine life, repairers of the earth, dancers with the Divine, community creators, and virtue restorers.

> At the root of every person . . .
> Notwithstanding the great blindness into which we've fallen,
> Notwithstanding the great slumber that has settled upon us,
> . . . We are, at our core, *of* God.
> Again, this has tremendous implications for the way we live.

A Better Story Changes Everything

When we rethink our story in this way, it changes the way we act in our communities, in both the community of faith and in the larger community around us.

When we see one another in the darkest times in life, in the throes of terrible failure, we interpret these dark times as veneer, not essence. The dark times are secondary, not primary. Our spiritual eyes always look past the failure, past the sin, to seek out the Divine Life within. Our role in the community is to act as partners on the spiritual journey drawing from one another the truest and deepest parts of ourselves.

This runs contrary to the instinct of many churches. When our story is that our deepest nature is the sin nature, our instinct is to contain, suppress, or punish the darkness.

A better story also changes how we raise our children. We teach them to look deeply within themselves for divine wisdom. We teach them to look past the surface experience of confusion, failure, or shortcoming. We teach them to define themselves by goodness radiating from something richer, deeper, and truer. We train them to seek out the indwelling Divine, listen for the inner voice, and trust the inner virtue present within them. Of course, we teach them to listen to us for a season, but ultimately, our training focuses on helping them listen to and honor the Deep within themselves.

A better story changes how we process our own failures. Even in the throes of our biggest disgraces, our most embarrassing breakdowns, it is *within* ourselves that we go for strength, healing, and restoration. We've always taught our children that Jesus is "in their hearts" and that the Spirit of God indwells them. The inward journey gives us access to divine healing, redemption, and restoration.

Finally, a better story of human nature changes the way we deal with people who hurt and repel us. So often our hurt at the hands of others happens because of our own blindness, our own twisted instincts, and our own interior darkness. Hurt, when our story speaks of the inner Divine, drives us inward to find peace, solace, wisdom, and our truest selves. We seek out the inner light of God to guide us, the presence of the Holy Spirit to redeem us and to afford us the wisdom, grace, peace, and love that are there inside us.

But we also do the same for one another. In our dark times, we encourage one another to go within, to find God's Spirit at our very centers. Our prayers for one another, the spiritual disciplines we teach one another, all focus on drawing one another toward the indwelling light of God. When our story tells us that human nature is divine first, and sinful second, it changes Christian community. It becomes our instinct to always seek awakening to the Light in ourselves and one another.

This expectation of the indwelling divine changes everything. What we look for we find. When we look for God's light in ourselves and others, it is there to be found.

Phillip Newell tells a story about the impact of changing what we look for.

> A number of years ago, I delivered a talk in Ottawa, Canada . . .
> I referred especially to the prologue of the gospel of John and his
> words concerning "the true light that enlightens everyone coming into the world" (John 1:9). I was inviting us to watch for that
> Light within ourselves, in the whole of our being, and to expect to
> glimpse that Light at the heart of one another and deep within the
> wisdom of other traditions.
>
> At the end of the talk, a Mohawk elder, who had been invited to
> comment on the common ground between Celtic Christianity and
> the native spirituality of his people, stood with tears in his eyes. He
> said, "As I have listened to these themes, I have been wondering
> where I would be today. I have been wondering where my people
> would be today. And I have been wondering where we would be as
> a Western world today if the mission that came to us from Europe
> centuries ago had come expecting to find the Light of God in us."[4]

4. Newell, *Christ*, 16.

If our starting point for thinking about human nature draws from the very opening scene of our story, "made in the image of God," and if our starting point is that the very stuff of God was breathed into us from the beginning, it changes everything!

A Better Story: We Belong Here!

The spirit-flesh split wasn't Jesus's idea. Jesus, Paul, and the Hebrew origins of our faith all reject the idea that we don't belong in the physical world. Rather, they teach us that we are in league with creation.

Romans 8 teaches a view of the earth and our place in it that is decidedly not Platonic or Gnostic. Listen to how Paul frames the world:

> All of creation waits in eager expectation for the sons [and daughters] of God to be revealed. For the creation was subjected to frustration, not by its own choice, but by the one who subjected it, but our hope is that creation itself will be liberated from its bondage to decay and brought into the glorious freedom that we, the children of God await. We know that the whole creation has been groaning as in the pains of childbirth right up to the present time.[5]

In this passage Paul suggests that there is a cosmic adventure afoot for *all* of creation. He tells us the entire created order waits with eager anticipation to be "set free from its bondage to decay." Paul's earth is not facing the painful ending of a terminal disease. No, the groans of creation are the groans of labor pain, the anticipation of a new birth.

This is not a vision of the material world about to be destroyed and dispensed with. Rather, it is a vision of humanity and creation journeying together toward a divine future purpose. Creation is not a departure point for the human spirit, but a traveler with us on the journey to divine eternity. The earth is not a booster rocket we leave behind as we soar off into our spiritual but not physical future. Paul is of the mind that creation comes with us! Whatever final disposition of time and space awaits, it awaits *all* of creation. Human beings and the material world are going on a journey together. Like us, the earth is moving forward into the great mystery before us. Paul's Christianity does not speak of the human spirit alone inheriting the purposes of God while the rest of the material world is destroyed. His story

5. Rom 8:19–21.

is that humanity and creation are on this journey together, both on their way to the fulfillment of a divine story, both on their way to a new reality.

It would be helpful if the Christian spirituality we give our children honored our Jewish heritage more than our Greek one. Jewish scriptures, interpreted by Jewish people, foster a voracious appetite for life in all of its material expressions. For them, the material world is to be savored and enjoyed, and in it, one can expect to find the sacred, the divine.

Listen to the writer of Ecclesiastes:

> I've looked at life from every angle, and this is what I come to
> . . . Enjoy the life you have. Eat your food with gladness, and drink
> your wine with a joyful heart, for it is now that God favors what
> you do. Always be clothed in white, (i.e. stay cool in the hot sun),
> and always anoint your head with oil (i.e. look and smell good).
> Enjoy life with your wife, whom you love, all the days of this . . .
> life that God has given you under the sun.[6]

This is a spirituality of belonging, not of alienation. It is a spirituality that feels at home in human culture, at home in nature, at home in commerce, and at home in politics. It is a spirituality that does not disdain human society, but seeks divine life and breath in the midst of it all. This is a spirituality that sees the broken and fouled parts of culture, of media, and of society not as the inevitable outcome of human corruption, but as parts of God's beloved creation in need of restoration.

This is a spirituality of recovering what has been lost, remembering what has been forgotten, and redeeming what has been broken. It is a spirituality of connectedness and belonging, a spirituality that shares kinship with the planet, and kinship with the people of the planet.

In the affirmation that all of creation exists and throbs with the energy of Divine Spirit, this spirituality grounds us in the physical-spiritual and gives us a part to play, a contributing part, a repairing part, a healing and restoring part. Our world is full of pain and injustice and Jesus calls us to heal it. To be connected to the earth is to belong in the midst of its beauty and to be part of redeeming its suffering. We belong to the earth; we belong to one another.

---

6. Eccl 9:1–10 (paraphrased excerpts).

Each person is my brother, my sister. Each person is mine to care about because I belong here.

I belong on this sacred earth, and I have a mission born of that belonging.

When I see the plight of the wounded, my story would *never* say; "There, there. It will be better when you get to heaven." No! It is to me to act as a conduit of the redeeming work of God for all of the cosmos. Mine may be a small role in the redemptive process, but the Divine has placed me here and made this my home. I am being redeemed while I live here, and at the same time I am about the business of redeeming the earth to which I belong.

It is natural then, that we followers of Jesus go about the family business of repairing and redeeming the earth. Of course we do! This is our home. This is our family. We belong here. We are salt, spread on the earth to preserve everything, for everyone. We are light, shining on the earth so everyone can be free of darkness.

This story helps us hear and resonate with the teachings of Jesus to engage with, heal, and care for society. Repairing the earth is not an afterthought, but the very centerpiece of Jesus's message on the kingdom of God.

When we see ourselves in the image of God . . .

When we see ourselves belonging on this earth . . .

Ours is not the religion of short-timers just passing through.

No! We are owners, stayers, engagers, and caregivers.

We *belong* here on God's good earth.

Rethinking Jesus

Divinity in a Human Body?

Warning: Them's Fightin' Words

Before we begin to think about Jesus, we should begin with a caveat. One of most contentious issues in Christianity's history has been the way we talk about Jesus, and particularly about the divinity of Christ. As our history has unfolded, battle lines have been drawn, and each successive generation has been assigned the job of defending them. More than any issue, what we believe about Jesus has been the litmus test that determines our fidelity to the faith: who is in and who is out. When I was a kid, "cult classes" were in vogue. We were working hard to determine which groups were "one of us" and which were not. The deciding factor always had to do with what each group believed about Jesus.

That's a lot of pressure. It's no small thing to take up a project on rethinking our story, if part of our story has to do with rethinking the divinity of Christ. While preparing this project, I was talking about it with a good friend, a devout Christian. As I talked about some of the topics our community was rethinking together, he grew increasingly uncomfortable. He wasn't rude, but we could see rude from where we were. "Go ahead and rethink these things if you must," he said, "but just make sure you leave the divinity of Christ alone. Some things are just too sacred to mess with!" There wasn't any wiggle room for rethinking. The topic was just off limits.

So here's the warning. If you want a donnybrook with your Christian friends, this is the way.

That being said, if we don't revisit our story and wring deeper understanding from it, even about its central character, our souls will continue to wither, and our religion will continue to decline. We *need* to rethink our instincts and feelings about the nature of Jesus and particularly the issue of divinity. As we'll see, some of our current instincts contradict the words of Jesus himself.

So, eyes wide open, here we go.

Mrs. Beale and My Junior High Sunday School Class

As a boy I was part of an irreverent discussion in my junior high Sunday school class. The topic was Jesus and bodily functions. A laughing group of eleven- to thirteen-year-olds were peppering our kind, older, church-lady teacher with questions about Jesus passing gas, vomiting, and other things that fascinate adolescent boys. I remember her laughing at us with kindness and tolerance. She obviously understood the age group. But I equally remember her adamant insistence that Jesus would never have had to deal with such embarrassing concerns. It was inconceivable to her that Jesus, the visible expression of the invisible God, could be reduced to a world of blood, semen, and gastric air. Her view of divinity insisted that the inexhaustible truth and beauty of the Divine could never exist in such proximity to bowels or foot odor.

I smile when I recall the camaraderie I felt with those boys so long ago, but in my old-man brain, I'm also sobered to think that our idea of the divinity of Jesus would be so sanitized, so divorced from the earthiness of human life.

Our tendency as Christians has been to do just that: to divorce divinity and humanity.

In 451 CE, the church held a council in the Turkish town of Chalcedon (near present-day Istanbul). At that council, after a lot of deliberation and debate, it was decided that the official Christian doctrine about Jesus would be that he was *fully human and fully divine*. That's our official position: *fully human, fully divine*. Those old bishops decided to leave us a legacy of paradox. They decided to leave our most contentious issue shrouded in contradiction. Jesus is as human as you and I are. And Jesus is divine.

Again, people tend to divorce divinity and humanity. We don't tend to imagine them as anything other than discrete, separate categories. Even though we made paradox the official Christian doctrine, we've still had a hard time marrying the two in our minds. Our discrete-category instincts run deep. Whatever human nature is, it is clearly *not* divine, and whatever divine nature is, it is clearly *not* human. Humanity and divinity feel as distinct from one another as the east is from the west.

This is the part of our story we need to rethink.

We now live in a world where subatomic particles can be in two places at one time.[1] Paradox is not the troubling issue it once was. We have instincts available to us that we did not have in the Enlightenment era.

I've spent my life helping Christians on the spiritual journey and have seen firsthand that rigidly compartmentalizing humanity and divinity harms us. The scriptures enjoin us to live as Jesus lived, to follow him, and to do the things he did.[2] We are to care for the sick, heal the wounded, confront injustice, and live selflessly. It is hard to take this mandate seriously when "Jesus is God" and we are not. Caught up in lives of bills, jobs, frailty, and foot odor, the temptation is to be overwhelmed by our own mortality.

Janet and Her Mother-In-Law

Janet's mother-in-law is wicked-mean. I've met her. She really is! To Janet's face, she plays syrupy sweet, but behind her back, she says awful things about her. Even face to face, her sweetness is laced with an undeniable sense of disapproval and slight. When Janet hears second-hand the awful things said about her, it hurts deeply. She has tried to be kind and caring toward the woman, but veiled criticism and rejection are her only reward. It has gotten so brutal that Janet avoids her whenever she can.

Jesus, on the other hand, while dying on the cross, looked at those crucifying him and prayed: "Forgive them, Lord. They don't know what they're doing."[3]

1. O'Callaghan, "*Superpositioning*," para. 24.
2. John 14:12.
3. Luke 23:34.

Janet knows that as a follower of Jesus, there is a calling on her life to emulate that same kind of grace, understanding, and forgiveness. But honestly! The woman is just awful!

It bothers her that she does not have the spiritual maturity to overcome her revulsion toward her mother-in-law. She would like to feel at least neutral toward the woman, perhaps even some degree of kindness and grace. But it's just not there.

In conversation, Janet and I were talking about the way the ancient spiritual practices help us in situations like this. Somewhere in the conversation, I used the term "like Jesus." Janet paused, sat back in her chair, and rolled her eyes. "Yeah," she said. "It'd be nice to be God, wouldn't it?"

The idea that Jesus was God, and therefore in a different category than herself, made the goal of "being like Jesus" seem a pipe dream, a wish-on-a-star fantasy. Christians hold that there is within us the same capacity to live deeply and virtuously that was in Jesus. However, it is difficult to imagine how that works when Jesus is God, and we are mortal. Jesus? Well he was just different!

Many Christians I know feel disconnected from Jesus. Following him doesn't inspire us to better lives because we see him in a separate category from ourselves. Believing he exists on a loftier plane than we do, we imagine him with access to resource that normal people don't have. Consequently, we unconsciously reduce Jesus to a figurehead in our religion, a symbol or mythic superhero. Rather than inspiring us, our Jesus-is-God instincts turn us into passive observers of our superhuman leader. It is difficult to be inspired to spiritual heights by someone who existed in a different category from ourselves.

Does "Divinity" Mean "Deity?"

To help us out of this impasse, we might ask ourselves what Christians mean when we say Jesus is "fully divine." Listening for the unconscious assumptions behind our language, it seems we treat "divine" as a synonym for "deity."

As a concept, divinity falls squarely in the category of ineffable things, things that cannot be talked about. So when we speak of Jesus being divine, at best we're scrambling to make meaning of an idea that cannot be contained.

It is an unconscious human tendency to try to reduce the irreducible concept of divinity into a framework or context that helps us contain it in our minds. And the idea of a deity works. We diminish the Christian idea of divinity when we do it, but "deity" is such a familiar construct it's worth the tradeoff. We know how to work with "deity."

The deity archetype has been around for thousands of years. It holds an old and comfortable position in our shared consciousness. Every ancient culture has at one time or another worshipped deities: superhuman, immortal beings that were part of our meaning-making narratives. We made them concrete beings in our minds so we could worship and revere them. Even though we reject the idea of deities today, they hold such a strong heritage in our collective minds that they provide a nice fallback position when we're trying to speak of unspeakable truths. When we cast about for a way to understand the unspeakable divine, the deity idea is right there, a shared cultural archetype.

The idea of Jesus being divine is similar enough to the idea of a deity that it works to link the two in our minds. We believe the spirit of Jesus is immortal; deities are immortal. We worship Jesus; people worship deities. Jesus had special powers; deities have special powers. The idea works.

Except that it doesn't.

When Christianity spread west, it encroached on the territory of the Greco-Roman gods. The Greeks worshiped Zeus. The Romans called him Jupiter. In the pantheon were Neptune, Mars, Apollo, and many others. These were deities that defined the genre; humanlike beings, but with a whole lot more power.

So when Christians determined that Jesus was special, we needed a mental box into which to put his specialness. The notion of a humanlike being with a whole lot more power worked. Jesus was kind of like you and me, but bigger and better, more powerful and capable, able to do things you and I could not do. He could walk on water, turn water into wine, and heal people. He looked like us but was clearly in a different category of existence.

While we never say it explicitly, many Christians think of Jesus's divinity very similarly to the way other cultures think of demigods. The Greeks had Heracles and Perseus. They were part human and part god. Again, we would never say it out loud, but our unspoken assumptions reveal too many parallels not to make the link.

Demigods are preternatural: humanlike, but possessing a status and abilities mortals do not. So was Jesus. In many cultures deities were immortal, beyond the reach of death. Jesus was, too. Demigods have strong, distinct personalities; remarkable birth narratives; and the ability to perform miracles and healings. Jesus did, too.

With such strong archetypes floating out there in our shared history, it is understandable that we would latch onto them to speak of Jesus. Our visceral instinct is to think of Jesus as a superhuman being. However, when we do, we undercut any meaningful way of thinking of Jesus as a human being like you and me.

Fully Human

The ideas of "deity" or "demigod" render the idea of "fully human" meaningless. Consequently, as concepts, they are too limited to contain the story of Jesus. Even though it is a comfortable mental box, it can't contain the full spectrum of meaning Christians assign to Jesus. It devalues the rich dimensionality of our mysterious, paradoxical faith. A deity cannot be human. Jesus is. A deity is not like you and me. Jesus is. A religious follower cannot aspire to be like a deity in any real way. Deities are not made of the same stuff we are. Jesus is.

Our scriptures insist that Jesus was the firstborn of many growing into the same expression of God-Life that he expressed.[4] A superman Jesus doesn't allow for such an idea. It makes it difficult to imagine aspiring to be second- or third-born supermen.

But if we explore the mysterious word "divine" more deeply, we can imagine a better story of Jesus.

In common usage, our dictionaries define "divine" three ways:

- having a character like God,
- a life lived in a God-like manner, or
- an existence that reflects God.

4. Rom 8:29.

Possessing a character like God, living a God-like life, or reflecting the nature of God. These ideas about Jesus's divinity make him a character we *can* aspire to follow. Made in the image of God, our own human nature points us to spiritual journeys just like his. Following Jesus points toward an ever-growing expression of divine character and virtue, toward lives spent emulating Jesus, the firstborn of many.

We ignore our own tradition when we make the difference between Jesus and ourselves a qualitative one. If our instinct about Jesus is that he existed in a completely different category than we do, then he's not human at all.

Christians believe that Jesus lived out the divine nature in a way that was unique, profound, and different from the way you and I live. However, that does not mean we have to think he did so because he possessed a nature that was essentially different from our own. Rather, we could think of this profound difference being a matter of degree; a quantitative, not a qualitative difference. Jesus expressed the divine at the highest level, but we can all express it at some level.

Instead of despair ("Yeah . . . it'd be nice to be God, wouldn't it?") when we frame Jesus as one of us, we see his deep expression of God's nature as an invitation, a call to aspire to ever more clearly express God's nature through our own humanity.

This is the story of the Christian scriptures. Our creation account tells us we each hold within ourselves the very nature of God. It tells us that like Jesus, we proceed *from* God and are made in the likeness of God. And yes, we carry a fallen nature, but the same essential nature exists in us that existed in Jesus.

When Christians experience Jesus, both today and long ago, we experience him as a reality bigger than ourselves. We glimpse in him something of the transcendent. He arouses in us a sense of divine presence that dwarfs our current experience. So for centuries, when we've had this glimpse of transcendence we have been, and continue to be, awed. We resonate with what Paul said about Jesus, that he shows us in a way we *can* contain, the God that we *cannot.*[5] We see in him a glimpse of the unspeakable transcendence that is contained in redeemed humanity.

5. Col 1:15.

But when we shoehorn that awe into the word "deity" we reduce it to a concept we know how to talk about. We reduce Jesus to something containable and put him in box that is too small. "Deity" diminishes Jesus, and diminishes our own spirituality in the process. When we settle for a deity we place the central figure of our faith outside human experience, removing him from the realm in which we live. Living outside the realm we live in, the realm of emotional upheaval, hurt, disappointment, and ecstasy, Jesus becomes the unapproachable "Son of God," rather than a figure that inspires us to follow him. Consider these words from the book of Hebrews:

> We don't have a priest who is out of touch with our reality. He [Jesus] has been through weakness and testing, experienced it all—all but the sin. So let's walk right up to him and get what he is so ready to give. Take the mercy, accept the help.[6]

A Digression: Three Layers of Human Consciousness

To help us think about Jesus, let's detour a moment and revisit human nature. In this digression I will suggest that our trouble imagining Jesus as fully human stems from a downgraded story about what it means to be human. Perhaps our instinct to reduce Jesus to a deity results from our tendency to focus too strongly on the sinful parts of human nature, to divorce human nature from its divine origins. As we've seen, influenced by Platonic dualism, we've tended to diminish our doctrine of *imago Dei*: made in the image of God, animated by the breath of God. On this side of Christianity's westward expansion, it is very difficult for us to think of human nature as being made of the same stuff God is.

Building on what we said about human nature, let me suggest a way of thinking about our humanity that will help us better tell the story of Jesus.

Body Consciousness

Human beings have bodies, and a way of being conscious that is associated with them. We are physically aware of heat and cold, hunger and thirst. Our bodies are aware of sleepiness, itchiness, and restlessness. The whole gamut of physical sensation inundates our every moment. We are conscious of

6. Heb 4:15–16 MSG.

existing in three dimensions, in time and space, aware of up and down and the gravity that defines them. We are sensitive to the boundaries in which we exist, in the skin package that contains us. We experience existing inside our skin in a different way than we experience existing outside it.

Body consciousness is rooted in physicality. It relies on our five senses to monitor external and internal environments. It distinguishes wakefulness from slumber and knows if we're energized or fatigued. It carries muscle memory and is conscious of mugginess or dryness.

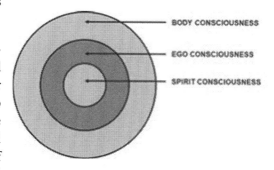

As we experience consciousness in this physical way there is another layer of awareness that is able to monitor the process. Some part of us is able to stand outside the experience of body consciousness and watch it happen. There is a part of me able to *observe* my hands feeling and my eyes seeing. I am able to experience both hot and cold, and at the same time watch myself experiencing it. "Hey, look at me feeling hot or cold," I can say.

Which invites the question: What part of me is able to watch myself being body conscious?

Ego Consciousness

We usually assume that the part of us that is able to watch over our bodies is the mind. Our minds are simultaneously able to direct *and* monitor the data our physical senses gather. The part of us that is able to think thoughts, feel feelings, have personality, and pursue plans is also able to monitor the consciousness we experience in our bodies. The mind, or the ego consciousness, is a complex part of us that serves a wide variety of functions. In addition to monitoring physical consciousness, it is able to express individual temperament, form habits, follow instincts, and generate a sense of right and wrong. It is so complex that it both misbehaves, *and* punishes us when it does. It is the place we create our morality, and then watch over ourselves to see how moral we're being.

In the ego layer of consciousness we are able to contemplate truth and beauty, and wonder what makes a good life. It is here that we experience ourselves as extroverts or introverts, where we possess preferences, strengths, and weaknesses.

Body consciousness monitors physical sensation. Ego consciousness thinks thoughts, feels feelings, *and* monitors body consciousness. At first glance, it could seem that these two layers of consciousness, understood deeply enough, would suffice to define our humanity. However, saints, sages, and students of the human condition insist we carry within ourselves a third layer of consciousness.

Observer Consciousness. Spirit Consciousness?

In the same way that ego consciousness can stand outside of body consciousness and watch it happen, there is also a part of us that can stand outside of ego consciousness and watch *it* happen. We have in ourselves the capacity to monitor our own minds and hearts, the ability to observe ourselves thinking thoughts and feeling feelings. We can watch ourselves being moral or immoral, extroverted or introverted, impulsive or methodical.

You can do it right now as you're reading this. You can both focus on the meaning of these words, and at the same time, watch yourself doing it. We have an internal mechanism that enables us to say, "Look at me feeling happy or sad," or "Look at me thinking thoughts about human consciousness."

As we dig deeply into ego consciousness we find layers beneath explicit awareness. Digging deeply into our own egos, we find plenty of material in the subconscious part of us. However, no matter how deeply we dig, once we get there that ability for interior monitoring remains with us. As we become aware of thought, feeling, or belief deep in our subconscious minds, the observing layer of consciousness is right there, able to stand outside and observe our newly unearthed awareness. No matter how deeply we dig into ego consciousness, there is another layer inside us able to monitor the process, and observe it happening.

At the center of our humanity there is a watcher, a looker, an observer.

Which raises the question: What is this part of me that can stand outside me and watch me?

We're Just Making This Stuff Up

It's a tough question to answer. As soon as we try to study this observing part of us—we *become* the observing part of us. When we look at the looking self—we *become* the looking self. When we watch the watching part of us—we *become* the watching part of us.

The layer of consciousness inside us that observes the other parts of us cannot itself be observed. When we observe it, we *become* it. We can experience *being* it but we can't dissect it, parse it out, study it, or define it. It is a mysterious layer of our humanity, an unknowable unknown at the center of who we are.

Through practice we become adept at experiencing this deep observing part of ourselves, but even so, we are unable to define exactly what it is. We can't pin down this part of ourselves with any kind of precision. It's there. We can *be* it. We just can't *study* it. It exists at a level deeper than body, deeper than mind, and deeper than temperament, instincts, thoughts, or feelings.

What is this mysterious inner observing self?

What is this mysterious inner part of me?

Philosophers, saints, and sages have puzzled over this question for a long time. Unable to clearly define the experience, we do the next best thing. We make stuff up.

Absent the ability to define this deep part of us, we do what human beings do to make meaning. We tell ourselves a story. We make something up. And of course, different people make up different stories.

Secularists make up that this part of our consciousness is nothing more than chemicals and electrons interacting deep inside our material, mechanical brains. Buddhists and Hindus make up that the observer self is a drop of universal consciousness traveling through space and time on its way back to the ocean of oneness that contains everything. The Abrahamic religions hold that God exists in a real way at the deepest level of who we are. We speculate that this observer nature within us somehow manifests the indwelling mystery of God.

Here's what we Christians make up. Unlike the secularists, we hold that the deepest part of us is not nothing. It is something; something precious and important. We teach our children that this deepest part of us is where the spirit of Jesus, the spirit of God, lives in our hearts. As we've seen, our creation narrative tells us we are animated by the very breath of God. We've also seen Jesus himself praying that we would experience our oneness with God as he did. When our tradition teaches us to walk after the Spirit, we believe it is from this deep part of us that we draw. When the fruit of the Holy Spirit is manifest in our lives, it is from this center that it flows.

Christians believe that at the deepest part of our humanity, we are made of the same stuff God is made of.

At the centermost part of us we carry the divine image. We carry the deep, divine, ineffable, and transcendent mystery. Unable to pin down the innermost part of ourselves any better than we can pin down or define God, our scriptures, saints, and contemplatives imagine that our inner observer self may in fact be a manifestation of the Divine within us. We have seen that we are able to experience God, but not define God. The same is true of our own deepest nature. We experience this silent, observing-self part of us as an expression of our divine centers: *of* God, *in* God, and made of the same mysterious, inaccessible, transcendent, ineffable stuff God is made of.

The Divinity of Christ

With this background, let's reconsider how Jesus might be fully human, how he might be like you and me and at the same time, fully divine.

If human nature contains the very nature of God, we could imagine Jesus carrying within himself the divine nature in the same way that every human being carries it within herself or himself. Once our story tells us the deepest part of human nature is *of* God, we can imagine Jesus's humanity quite naturally carrying divinity.

I can imagine Christians reacting negatively to this idea. I can imagine many feeling that it somehow diminishes Jesus's divinity. However, rather than seeing this story diminishing Jesus's divinity, we could see it elevating the nature of his humanity. In this story, ours becomes the belief that human nature carries, as a matter of course, the same essential divine nature that Jesus carried.

The specialness that distinguishes Jesus from the rest of humanity then, is not that he was divine and we are not. In this way of telling our story, we *all* carry within ourselves the same divine nature Jesus did. What distinguishes Jesus from normal, everyday people is not his divinity, but how purely he *expressed* that divinity. This telling of our story both honors the divine nature embedded in humanity *and* allows Jesus to be the standard-setter for all of us. In this telling, Jesus shows us what it looks like for human beings to live from the divine center. In this story, rather than being a totally different, non-human being, Jesus is an expression of what it means to be fully human.

Illusion and the False Self

Let's look again at the layers of human consciousness and include an element left out earlier: illusion. The experience is universal. Ego consciousness does not exist in an unadulterated state. It is not a well from which we draw only virtue, decency, and righteousness. No, ego consciousness also holds within it dark nodules of illusory belief, undigested hurt, and unhealed wounds. Imagine these

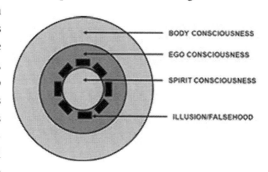

dark soul wounds littered throughout our ego generating their own thoughts and feelings. Imagine these falsehoods, these wounds, these illusions generating everyday actions, feelings, instincts, drives, and impulses.

Many of us, at the deepest levels of ego consciousness hold beliefs like these:

- "I am not worthy of love."
- "I have been so bad, I have to earn any love I get."
- "There is not enough in the world for me. Others get what they need, but not me."

Core beliefs like these generate an internal response. They generate thoughts, actions, and eventually life strategies. If I believe myself un-precious, of course I claw and fight to earn my preciousness. Core illusions generate all kinds of subconscious impulses, conscious thoughts and physical responses.

They generate a whole bevy of strategies designed to protect us from our frightening beliefs, keep us safe, and control the dangerous world.

- "I will earn my preciousness by getting people to like me, come hell or high water."
- "I will convince myself of my worth by earning more money than the next guy."
- "I will make myself safe by controlling all the people, circumstances, and variables in life."

Eventually, these illusion based strategies take over our lives. They become our instincts. They become so embedded in our lives that they eclipse our divine, spirit consciousness center. Interior illusions so deeply color the way we interpret and live life, that they eventually generate a version of self. Rooted in these dark nodules of false belief and illusion, our reactionary strategies, instincts, and feelings eventually become the "us" from which we live.

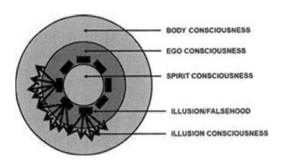

The illusion based version of self doesn't flow from the divine center but from lesser, false truths; distorted reality; and wounded perceptions. It is a false version of self. However, though it is false, it is the only self we believe we have. Consequently, it is powerful. It has its own vested interest in sticking around. Founded on illusion, this lesser self nevertheless strives to survive. It has to. It believes it is the only "me" there is. However, its instincts are rooted in illusion, not in the divine center. Consequently, these instincts often betray us. They cause us to zig when we should zag. They cause us to unwittingly fracture our relationships. We tend to forgive when we should stand for justice. We exact a pound of flesh when we should extend grace. In our personal lives, we wound those we love. On the global stage, we go to war. Believing this false, illusion based version of self is the real self, we create and experience no end of human misery.

A corrupted, polluted, and contaminated ego creates strategies for living that become so loud and insistent, they drown out the divine center. They crowd out truth based instinct. They shout down the quiet divine voice that indwells us.

We live. But we live divorced from our true, divine-image selves.

Jesus: Illusion Free and Fully Human

With this in mind, one way to think of Jesus's life is as a purified expression of true, authentic humanity. His was a life free of the illusion-based false self. Jesus stands apart in history, having walked the earth as a *true* human, absent the false belief, illusion, and toxic instinct that so infect the human condition.

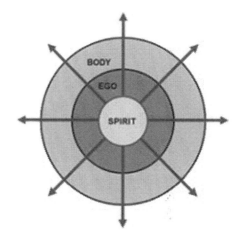

Paul said it like this: "Jesus knew no sin."[7] The author of Hebrews said he was tempted in every way we are, but navigated the human experience without sin.[8]

True, unadulterated humanity, unencumbered by the illusion and soul wounds from which we construct our false selves, is able to express the divine center without hindrance. That is Jesus. Fully human. Fully divine.

Instead of thoughts, feelings, words, and deeds emanating from the hurts and misbeliefs that characterize the illusory human experience, Jesus lived as humans are created to live, from the divine center. Jesus radiated the essence of God that indwells us all, unblocked, unpolluted, unadulterated by the coping strategies that so ensnare and divide us from our own divine center, spirit consciousness.

In this way of telling our story, what distinguishes Jesus from the rest of us is not his divine nature, but his freedom from the sin nature that shouts down our divine natures. In his pure humanity, Jesus expressed the divine without distortion.

7. 2 Cor 5:21.
8. Heb 4:15.

And when he did, we stood in awe, and said, "He is divine!"

But Jesus wasn't content just to be divine. Having demonstrated what true humanity looks like, he invited all of us to share in his experience; to do what he did, and even greater things; and to live from the same divine center he did.[9]

If we tell the story of Jesus's divinity existing *within* his humanity, we don't disconnect ourselves from his life. Janet wouldn't have to wistfully wish she could respond to her mother-in-law with the same wisdom and spirituality Jesus demonstrated. Rather, she could look to Jesus, and be inspired to seek out the same divine center from which Jesus lived.

We carry within ourselves the same divine presence that was in Jesus. We acknowledge his difference from ourselves, but it is a quantitative one, not a qualitative one. Our divine centers may be hidden under dark splotches of falsehood, instinct, and woundedness, but Jesus inspires us to be set free, to be healed and delivered, so we can live from our own divine essence.

Our texts tell us Jesus showed us what the divine nature looks like in a human being.[10] He showed us what is possible in our lives, demonstrating the divine that is embedded in our humanity, at the core of our truest selves. And in the showing, he calls us to new life, an abundant and holy life, awakened to the divine presence inside us. It is a call to life beyond illusion, beyond sin nature, and beyond the false self.

When our story engenders the expectation that Jesus's essential nature is ours as well, we experience salvation as a call back to our truest state, back from the place to which we have fallen, back to our identity as expressions of God, and back to lives lived in the image of God.

As we'll see in the next section, two Christianities emerge from two stories about Jesus. Our stories of sin and salvation are very different depending on which Jesus we follow. When we regard Jesus as a different kind of being than we are, salvation is a passive affair. We have no choice but to wait help-lessly until we are rescued from our corrupt human nature. However, when our story tells that Jesus was *like* us, that God's nature indwells us just as it

9. John 14:12.

10. Col. 1:15.

did him, salvation is no longer a struggle against our separation from God. It is no longer about gaining access to a distant and displeased God.

As we'll see, access to God can never be lost. That's not what salvation is about. Rather, Christian salvation is about waking up to our truest, God-image selves. It is not, as so many have been taught, about praying the right prayer so we can get back into relationship with God. No! Forgiveness and relationship with God are never lost. Our salvation story isn't about *doing something* to change God's posture toward us. Rather, it is about removing the blinders to see what is already true. God's presence is in us. God, whose very nature is forgiveness and acceptance, is as close to us as close can be, inside our very selves. We can no more lose relationship with the Divine than we can lose our very selves.

This story of Jesus's divinity invites us to a spiritual journey of recovery, a quest to discover and return to our true, Jesus-like selves. Our story invites us to awaken to the indwelling spirit of God the way Jesus did. It invites us to access our own divine centers and live in a responsive dance with the life of God within us, the way Jesus did.

9

Following Jesus the Man

The High Cost of Ignoring Jesus's Humanity

When my children were younger, I "ruined" their summers by insisting that they read a significant book each year. One book I had them read was a collection of stories about young people setting right what is wrong in the world, fighting injustice, resisting poverty, and working against child labor and human trafficking.[1]

When they were finished, I asked each child to my office to talk it over. "Why do you think I had you read that book this summer?" I asked. They stumbled trying to get the right answer so they could get on with their summers. I particularly remember my son Daniel answering with a series of canned Sunday school responses. To each of his responses, I'd reply, "Nope, that's not why I had you read the book." Finally, semi-joking, he pulled out all his best church answers. "I don't know exactly what you're looking for here, but I'm pretty sure the answer has to be either, 'God loves me,' 'Jesus saves me,' 'the Bible tells me,' or 'we should pray about it.'"

I laughed, and let him off the hook. "Daniel, I wanted you to read this book about people serving the earth, healing what is wounded, and fixing what is broken, because *this* is your religion. If you're a follower of Jesus, *this* is your religion.

"Jesus's message had very little to do with what happens after we die," I continued. "This book was about the real heartbeat of Jesus's teachings. People

1. Kielberger and Kielberger, *Me to We.*

healing the earth. People caring for others. When Jesus used the term 'The kingdom of God,' he was talking about the stuff people are doing in this book. 'Be salt, spread across the earth to bring out the God flavors,' he said. 'Be light, spread across the earth to show forth God's colors.'[2] 'Heal what is wounded.' 'Restore what is lost.' 'Challenge what is evil.' 'Enlighten what is blinded.' 'Repair what is broken.'

"This, Daniel . . . *this* is your religion."

Those times in history when we've given adequate attention to the humanity of Jesus have been times we Christians have been at our best. When we followed Jesus, a human being like you and me, we have been inspired to resist slavery, create hospitals, and make sure there was education and food for everybody.

Jesus, the human being, taught us to better the earth. He was an opponent of injustice and a provocateur. He resisted oppression and fought for right over wrong. As his followers, ours is to take up the mantle and advocate for the well-being of the earth.

Bettering the earth is the religion of those who follow the human Jesus.

When we only focus on the divinity of Jesus, we tend to become other-worldly. Ours becomes an inordinate focus on getting people right so they can get to heaven. We tend to deemphasize the pain and suffering of this world because our eyes are set on a better world in the afterlife. It is not the Christian way to care *less* about this world and the needs of people in it. This debases our heritage. It ignores most of what Jesus taught us.

We pay a heavy price when we deemphasize the human Jesus. It makes our spirituality anemic, and our souls vulnerable to all kinds of foolishness. Unhealthy, the voice we project to the world sounds shrill and fraudulent. People know Jesus taught selfless love for all. People know the followers of Jesus are to care for others. So when our instincts betray us, and our focus shifts toward moralizing, converting, and getting people to heaven, people recognize us for the frauds we become. When our lives are so different from the life of Jesus, how can they think anything else?

> I like your Christ. I do not like your Christians.
> Your Christians are so unlike your Christ.[3]

2. Matt 5:13–16.
3. Stroud. "Knights," 162.

Jesus under Roman Imperialism

Human beings exist in a specific time and place, the details of which profoundly define their lives. To understand my life, you would have to understand the American consumerist culture in which I live. You would have to understand twenty-first century science and technology and the economic forces I live with every day. You would need to know these things, and then measure how I respond to and interact with them.

Understanding the fully human Jesus is no different. Cultural and historical forces shaped Jesus's everyday life just as they do yours and mine. His teaching, mission, values, and priorities are incomprehensible if we do not understand the backdrop against which they unfolded. Those who take seriously the call to follow Jesus can't fully embrace his teaching or follow his example without awareness of the circumstances he was addressing. His culture gave his teaching its meaning. The social conditions in which he lived give explanation to his actions and words. Without these insights his followers become quite lost.

It is difficult to exaggerate the significance of Roman occupation in understanding Jesus's life. In the years immediately preceding his birth, Rome was transitioning from republic to empire. Julius Caesar had been appointed permanent dictator in 44 BCE. The Roman Senate's power was diminishing, and as an empire, territorial expansion through conquest and colonization was ramping up, peaking shortly after Jesus.

Rome practiced the worst kind of imperialism. Like all of Rome's colonies, Palestine was exploited ruthlessly. The bulk of the population was displaced, made landless, alienated, and enslaved. Impoverished and unemployed, subsistence farmers staggered under the heavy weight of double taxation. An agricultural tax went directly to Rome after each harvest on top of the normal tax to support the local puppet government. Tax policy was an unruly soup of unjust valuations, extortion, and blackmail. There was runaway inflation and colonists were regularly conscripted against their will to labor for their Roman overlords.[4]

This quote is widely attributed to Gandhi, but sources are disputed. He is quoted directly in "Knights:" *"I don't reject Christ. I love Christ. It's just that so many of you Christians are so unlike Christ."*

4. Kretzmann, *"Roman Government,"* para. 5.

It was a time of despotic rule and deep resentments. Jesus, the human being, was born right in the middle of this tumult. We miss his message if we don't see how it was informed by this great social and political upheaval. The role Jesus played in his society was shaped by the Roman occupation and the Jewish response to it.

Palestine was unique among Roman colonies in that its religious history was so powerfully deterministic. The way Jews thought of themselves was defined by their religious heritage. In their minds, they were a people, chosen by God, blessed by God, and called by God to be a blessing to all nations.[5] Theirs was a religion of divine promise. They expected protection, prosperity, and sovereignty as long as God was their God. So, when Rome ravaged their land, they were understandably gripped by the question of why God had abandoned them. What had happened to God's promise of protection? Why had God allowed Rome to dominate them so thoroughly, so humiliatingly, and so cruelly? Why hadn't God kept the promise made to their ancestors?

These chronic, troubling, and insistent questions were in the air, in the water, everywhere. Their urgency became the framing context into which Jesus was born. They framed his message and his life.

Roman occupation was unraveling Jewish society, with one point of upheaval being particularly galling. For centuries before the Roman invasion, Jewish society had developed a special kind of social cohesion. Founded on mutuality and care for one another, a special bond of community had evolved that prioritized kinship, codifying laws that strengthened and supported the well-being of the whole community. Laws prohibited citizens from taking excessive advantage of one another, and kept them from creating a perpetual upper and lower class.

People are born with unequal abilities. That's just the way things are. Some are born with more capacity, ambition, or energy; others with less. Some are able to manage their affairs better, others not well at all. Consequently, one person's capacity leads to prosperity; another person's leads to poverty. And when this happens, the most natural thing for those who come out on top is to try to pass their privileged position on to their children.

There are deeply ingrained patterns in the way human societies develop. When one group gains advantage in a society, the most natural thing in the

---

5. Gen 12:1–3.

world is for them to use that advantage to gain further advantage, and to pass it on to their children. You know how it goes. It takes money to make money. After enough generations work this system, the haves tend to create a system that keeps them having and keeps the have nots having not. Caste systems tend to evolve in which, despite ability, the children of the poor remain poor, and the children of the rich remain rich.

But Jewish society had resisted this pattern. Social laws worked against the creation of a permanent class system. The status of any one generation was not to be passed along to successive generations.

Jewish law afforded an incompetent or unfortunate generation a means of social security. Citizens were allowed to sell themselves into indentured servitude. A more capable neighbor could buy their land and labor, and the less capable could work the land as sharecroppers. In this way competent and incompetent alike could work, be fed, and survive. However, the children of the indentured generation were not to remain in servitude. Every forty-nine years, the land once sold was returned to the original family. Freedom, once surrendered, was returned. Jewish law codified a means of survival for those unable to manage life and land, but it did not create perpetual castes of haves and have nots.[6]

In the time of Jesus, however, this ancient social system was being dismantled. Under Roman occupation, Jews were adopting the class system of their conquerors. A handful of Jews were appointed as puppet rulers by Rome, and they began to perpetuate Roman class systems and dismantle the egalitarian laws of Jewish society. Exploiting the desperation created by heavy taxation, those who prospered under Roman occupation took advantage of their subsistence farmer neighbor's inability to pay. They swooped in, paid late taxes, and took permanent deed to ancestral lands. Old laws were disregarded and a new, permanent class system was imposed. High priests, wealthy landowners, and merchants began to live in great splendor, while most of the population was destitute.[7]

This social tinderbox was the backdrop of Jesus's life and teaching. This was the upheaval that shaped his life, message, and public dealings. Jesus's message was forged in the seismic shift going on in Jewish national identity, and

---

6. Lev 25:39.

7. Harris, "*Cows, Pigs*," 68.

was a response to the resentments fracturing national cohesion. And under this social pressure, questions of identity came front and center:

- "Are we God's people or not? Have we been abandoned?"
- "Why is Rome so powerful while we're so weak?"
- "What went wrong? Was it us? Did we do something?"
- "Shall we kill Roman collaborators or merely shun them?"

In response to these primal questions of identity, Jews formulated several different responses. The Zealots believed that it was Israel's complacency that was to blame for Roman occupation. They advocated a strong response of aggression and military action. Believing God helps those who help themselves, theirs was the cry, "Let's get 'em boys! If we do our part, God will do his. To arms! God will send us a heroic messiah to lead us to victory."

The Pharisees responded differently. They believed God had abandoned Israel because of sin and would come to their aid only if they got their act together. Theirs was a focus on challenging bad behavior. They scrupulously and meticulously followed all the religious codes, and castigated those who did not. They had to. The fate of the nation was at stake. Their strategy was to get tough on drunks, whores, gluttons, and the Jews who collaborated with the Romans. They thought, "Once we get these rascals into shape, God will come to our aid and send us the promised messiah to lead us to victory."

The Herodians weren't nearly as hopeful as either the Zealots or the Pharisees. They didn't really believe anybody could beat the Romans. Their posture was an old one: "If you can't beat 'em, join 'em! Go along to get along." They ran the puppet government for Rome, and became the tax collectors and land managers for the new landlord class.

I suspect they didn't see themselves as collaborators, but more as pragmatic realists. In private, they quite likely still held the Jewish narrative as a personal and private belief. But in public, they worked with and for Rome. They probably believed their collaboration was short-term, practical, and necessary. But in private, they too held the Jewish belief that if God ever did get around to answering their prayers, he'd send the promised messiah to lead them to victory.

All three of these responses to Roman occupation shared an underlying expectation. Jewish freedom would be finally realized only when God sent a messiah to lead them to victory. This became the dominant element in shaping the way Jewish people perceived and experienced Jesus.

Jesus and the Role of Warrior Messiah

Jewish expectation was that God would send a messiah to save them from their predicament. It was not, however, an expectation that this messiah would be a prince of peace. Not at all. Theirs was an expectation of a military, warrior deliverer. Theirs was an expectation that a messiah would return David's kingdom to them. Under David's military leadership, the boundaries of Israel had extended further than ever before or after. David had protected the nation from occupation, defeated its enemies, fought great battles, and overcome great cities. So of course the return of military supremacy was their expectation.

They came by this expectation honestly, even biblically. The Hebrew Scriptures are filled with promises of such a messiah. The writings of the prophets all raise expectations of a promised military leader. Isaiah promised the messiah would "tread down Assyria, like mire in the streets."[8] He had similar expectations for enemies from Babylon and Moab,[9] Damascus, and Egypt.[10] Jeremiah threatened the Philistines, the Amorites, and the Moabites that once a messiah (a "Branch of Righteousness" he called him) grew up, he would execute judgment and righteousness upon Israel's enemies.[11]

In Jewish society, warrior messiahs had been showing up in the years before and after Jesus with varying degrees of success. Fed by prophetic promise, guerrilla uprisings regularly cascaded through their history, always enjoying popular support. These uprisings sought to restore Jewish independence, eliminate social and economic inequity, and overturn exploitive systems of political and economic colonialism. Under the particularly cruel system of Roman oppression, Jewish ire was intensely worked up. Fueled by injustice, cruelty, and a sense of divine promise, guerilla warriors had long been waging a prolonged struggle against the Roman system and the Roman army.

Josephus, an extra-biblical historical source about Jesus's time, reported regular uprisings in which absentee landlords and tax collectors were beaten.

8. Isa 10:5–6.
9. Isa 15:1–4.
10. Isa 17:1–3.
11. Jer 23:1–6.

Messianic leaders instigated skirmishes of harassment, robbery, assassination, and terrorism. Josephus chronicled at least five campaigns led against Rome by warrior messiahs from 40 BCE to 73 CE and indicated that there were many more he hadn't mentioned.[12]

Josephus helps us understand that the warrior messiah was a recognized genre of leadership in Jewish society, and that Jews had both a clear expectation and an established experience of this category of leader.

We cannot understand Jesus, the human being, without understanding the yearnings, longings, and objectives assigned to the genre of messiah leader. Jesus lived his life framed by these national hopes. His life and message were defined by the expectations of this kind of social, political, and military leader. This category of rebel leader in Jesus's time, defined Jesus himself.

How Jesus Fit the Role: The Warrior Messiah

Like all his countrymen, Jesus was anti-imperialism, anti-Rome, and anti-occupation. His life and message were rooted in Jewish resistance to Roman occupation and a sense of betrayal toward those countrymen who were collaborating with the occupiers.

The people living in Jesus's time, everyone from his followers to Jewish social and religious leaders, all interpreted Jesus's words and actions through the lens of messianic expectations. And Jesus did not disappoint them. Much of his teaching and many of his actions were exactly what one would expect of the traditional messianic leader. To understand how deeply Jesus fit the role of warrior messiah we need to understand both John the Baptist and the Qumran community. Qumran was a prophetic desert commune intently focused on gaining Jewish independence and freedom.

John the Baptist: Qumranic Prophet

The Dead Sea Scrolls, discovered in the 1940s and 50s, were the collected writings of the Qumran desert commune. The scrolls gave us new understanding of the ancient world and in particular, Jewish messianic expectations. From them scholars have been able to unravel the Qumran community's prophetic belief and appreciate how closely Jesus fit their expectations for

12. Harris, *Cows, Pigs,* 171–72.

the unfolding of Jewish history. Theirs was an expectation that Israel was heading toward an Armageddon. Rome would meet its doom and be replaced by a Jewish empire with Jerusalem as its capitol. They prophesied that a military messiah descended from David would rule and be mightier than any Caesar had ever been.

The scrolls tell us that Qumran sent missionaries to the Jews to prepare the way for the Coming One. These missionaries ate locusts and wild honey, and wore the skins of animals. Their job was to call the people of Israel to repentance, thus preparing the way for the coming empire of Israel.[13] In 68 CE, as Rome came to destroy Qumran, they sealed their library in jars and hid them in remote caves where they remained undisturbed until the twentieth century.

That John the Baptist wandered the desert dressed as he did tells us his life and mission are best understood within Qumranic tradition. His phrase "chaff burned in unquenchable fire"[14] is the same language the Qumranites used when they spoke about Rome's inevitable demise. When John uses these same words, wears the same clothes, eats the same food, it positions him within the community, and gives us a lens for interpreting his words. John's sociopolitical aspirations were Qumranic aspirations.

John was one of the holy men Josephus described wandering the badlands of the Jordon Valley, stirring up the peasants and making trouble for Rome and the Jewish collaborators. His career directly mirrored the desert prophets of Qumran. When he was killed, the gospels say it was for criticizing the puppet-governor Herod for marrying the divorced wife of one of his brothers. That may have been the spark that ignited the fire, but the fuel was his agitating role in the shooting war going on between Jews and Romans. John was stirring up growing crowds with preaching that was pure threat. His warning might have been: "A military messiah is coming! Rome! Herod! You better be ready!"

> One mightier than me is coming, and He will baptize you in spirit and fire: his winnowing fork is in his hand, and he will thoroughly cleanse his threshing-floor, and gather the wheat into his barn; but the chaff he will burn up with unquenchable fire.[15]

13. Ibid., 174.
14. Matt 3:12.
15. Matt 3:11–12.

Jesus as Apocalyptic Messiah

The Dead Sea Scrolls also help us understand Jesus. Like John, he too fit within Qumranic aspirations. John inspired an expectation of freedom and a coming hero to lead his people to that freedom. Jesus stepped up to be that hero. We cannot understand Jesus apart from the hopes of the people for a Jewish, apocalyptic messiah.

Jesus started his ministry with John the Baptist's people. Two of his disciples (Andrew and Peter) had previously been followers of John.[16] When Herod encountered Jesus, after he had beheaded John, he saw so little difference between Jesus and John that he remarked, "It is John, whom I beheaded. He is risen from the dead."[17] Like John, Jesus began his ministry wandering the back country where his miracles and powerful message drew such crowds that he had to keep moving in order to stay one step ahead of the priest police.

That Jesus willingly stepped into the messianic role helps us understand his intentions. Like the community around him, it was Jesus's intent to precipitate change in the social order. That's what prophets and warrior messiahs did. Like them, he was contending for a divinely directed downfall of unjust power structures. His posture toward Rome and its puppet government was clearly one of resistance.

When Jesus rode into Jerusalem on a donkey, we think of it as a peaceful symbol. What could be more humble and peaceful than a donkey? But to Jews, it invoked the prophesy of Zechariah:

> Rejoice greatly, O daughter of Zion! Shout in triumph, O daughter of Jerusalem! Behold, your king is coming to you; He is just and endowed with your salvation, He is humble, and mounted on a donkey, even on a colt, the foal of a donkey. I will cut off the chariot from Ephraim, and the horse from Jerusalem; and the bow of war will be cut off. He will speak peace to the nations; and His dominion will be from sea to sea, from the River to the ends of the earth.[18]

16. John 1:35–40.
17. Mark 6:16.
18. Zech 9:9–10.

A seemingly peaceful act of riding into Jerusalem on a lowly donkey was in fact an act of direct provocation. This was not gentle Jesus, meek and mild. This was a descendant of David, emboldened by the prophetic expectations of his people, rising from weakness to resist the chariots of Rome. This was an act of direct confrontation to the Roman Empire. And to these expectations, the people sang: "Blessed be the one who comes in the name of the Lord. Blessed be the son of David."[19]

Befitting the messianic role, Jesus's first act upon entering the city was to provoke a fight. He fashioned a whip, stormed the temple, and physically attacked those licensed by Rome to exchange currencies in the temple. He drove out the collaborators who were profiting on the backs of Jewish citizens. That's what warrior messiahs do.

Because Jesus was looking and speaking the part of warrior messiah, the political religious establishment clearly understood him in the role. From the time Caiaphas saw him attack the money changers, he plotted to arrest Jesus. He looked for a way and a time to put him away without interference from the mob who thought of him as their advocate, their deliverer, a descendent of David come to set them free. Caiaphas told the police to arrest Jesus, but not on a feast day when the mob was around to witness it, "or there may be a riot among the people."[20]

As Jesus played the part of warrior messiah, his disciples played the part of a warrior troop. Simon was a Zealot.[21] James and John were "Boanerges," meaning "sons of thunder."[22] These were the boys who wanted to call down fire on a Samaritan village because people hadn't welcomed Jesus. The disciples carried swords because Jesus taught them to, saying, "If you don't have a sword, you better sell your coat to get one."[23]

The life Jesus lived, the band he formed around himself, and the words he spoke all fit him neatly into the military messiah expectations of his people and his times.

---

19. Matt 21:9–10.
20. Matt 26:4–5.
21. Luke 6:15.
22. Mark 3:17.
23. Luke 22:36.

> Don't think I have come to bring peace to earth.
> No, I have not come to bring peace, but to bring a sword.[24]
> Do you think I have come to give peace to earth?
> I am telling you not, but rather to bring division.[25]

How Jesus Subverted the Role: The Anti-Messiah

But on the other hand . . .

Having used the messianic genre to establish his credentials, Jesus played the role in a way that also deviated from people's expectations. In fact, he used the role to subvert the role. Yes, Jesus was a warrior messiah, but he was also a Prince of Peace. Yes, Jesus was in the business of resisting Rome and establishing justice, but he was also in the business of subverting the people's expectations of how it would happen.

The Christian Scriptures seem conflicted when they describe Jesus. Was he a warrior or a peacemaker?

- On the one hand Jesus said he did not come to bring peace, but the sword.[26]

- On the other hand, he taught that those who make peace are blessed.[27]

- On the one hand, violence was a recurring theme for Jesus.[28]

- On the other hand, he taught people struck on one cheek to turn the other.[29]

- On the one hand, Jesus drove collaborating money changers out of the temple with a whip.[30]

- On the other hand, he taught people to love their enemies, and to do good to those who hated them.[31]

    So, was Jesus a warrior messiah, or a peaceful prince?

24. Matt 10:34.
25. Luke 12:51.
26. Matt 10:34.
27. Matt 5:9.
28. Matt 11:12.
29. Matt 5:40–41.
30. John 2:15.
31. Luke 6:27.

As a messiah, clearly, Jesus intended to bring justice to the oppressed as was expected. He was firmly rooted in the tradition of resistance to oppression, working on behalf of the downtrodden, the demoralized, and the oppressed. As messiahs do, he championed the cause of the exploited and resisted the power of exploiters.

However, while he placed himself firmly *within* the role, again and again he said and did things to undermine everyone's expectations *about* the role. As messiah, Jesus never questioned that justice was to be achieved, but he overturned everyone's expectations about *how* it would be. The role of messiah came loaded with expectations of military might and retributive violence, both of which Jesus transcended and subverted.

While Jesus's message was a clear call to resist injustice, doing so with violence and hatred just didn't work. "You can live by the sword if you like," he said, "but if you do, you will die by it. You may cut some Roman throats, but in the end they'll hate you all the more for it, and you can be sure they'll be back to cut yours."[32]

Jesus subverted the warrior messiah role by advocating new ways, different ways, better ways, to resist injustice. His subversive strategy was revolutionary: gain the heart of one's adversary. Retribution only perpetuates retribution. Alienation only perpetuates alienation. Jesus used the role of the messiah to advocate a better way.

Jesus, the man, thought creatively about solutions to intractable problems. Jesus was bent on achieving justice and peace, but not bogging down in old, defunct strategies. He envisioned a world in which evil was challenged, but people were not harmed in doing so. His was a strategy to awaken people to the divine way, the divine truth, and the divine life, and in so doing, to see them set free. His was an approach that focused on healing, redemption, and forgiveness to create peace. His was a strategy of changing the game by returning good for evil. Through the centuries when people have given Jesus's strategies a chance, they have proven to be effective. They are more difficult and take much longer, to be sure. In the short run they seem to extend the pain and suffering of those who do not lash out. However, once a new system is established, it creates a lasting peace.

---

32. Matt 26:52.

Hard-nosed pragmatists think Jesus's strategy naïve. In the face of the enormous load of evil on the earth, turning the cheek seems idealistic foolishness. However, these pragmatists may not have fully considered the alternative. Violence perpetrates violence. We may throw off the shackles of injustice with violent resistance, but not for long. When we fight violence with violence, we breed violence into our instincts, into the heart of our enemies. Jesus clearly understood that oppression breeds oppressors. Even when unjust systems remain in place for a long time, hurt people eventually get their revenge. Oppressed people eventually wiggle free, and when they do the cycle of alienation, division, hatred, and violence just doesn't stop.

An Eye for an Eye, And Soon The Whole World Is Blind

Gandhi was a fervent follower of Jesus. He wasn't a Christian man, primarily because his experiences of Christians were so bigoted and hurtful. But Gandhi followed Jesus, the man. He recognized the similarity between the position the Jews were in under Roman occupation and the Indians under British colonial rule. While he faced tremendous pressure from his countrymen to use violence to throw off British imperial exploitation, he challenged these instincts. Inspired by the teachings of Jesus, he insisted on a strategy of resistance, challenge, and overcoming, but without violence or hatred. He insisted on a strategy to gain justice today that would not create more oppression and hatred tomorrow. Nonviolent resistance takes longer, but once established, it lasts much longer.

Martin Luther King, Jr. advocated the same. In his last speech, *"I've Been to the Mountaintop,"* he assessed the struggle against segregation in Birmingham, Alabama. He spoke of mace, dogs, fire hoses, and hatred. But rather than returning hatred for hatred, the protesters prayed and sang. King described the sense of solidarity and strength their attitude created:

> And every now and then we'd get in jail, and we'd see the jailers looking through the windows being moved by our prayers, and being moved by our words and our songs. And there was a power there which Bull Connor couldn't adjust to.[33]

King always insisted that nonviolence was the only way to true victory. Violence and hatred might defeat one's adversary, but even so, all that kind of victory would do would be to reverse the players while maintaining the same

---

33. King, *"Mountaintop,"* para. 21.

toxic power dynamic. In his speech, he spoke to people for whom violence and hatred were attractive options. These visceral reactions are always attractive to the victims of injustice. The struggle in Birmingham had employed the weapons of the kingdom of God. Theirs was a strategy of righteousness, kindness, and the respect of dignity. They agitated for change, but respected their adversaries. They sang to the police as dogs were set on them, and they prayed for their adversaries when they turned on the hoses. In the long run they did not simply desegregate busses in Birmingham. Theirs was the larger mission to change the heart of the nation, to get *everyone* to see what justice required, to get *everyone* to be a willing partner in doing right.

In the messiah role, Jesus contended for justice and righteousness. Subverting the role, however, he called his followers to a more difficult path, a more thorough path. Purity codes wouldn't work. Collaboration for personal gain wouldn't work. Hatred and reactionary violence wouldn't work either.

Gandhi and Martin Luther King captured Jesus's two-pronged message. They successfully fought for justice, but did so in a way that didn't perpetrate a system of winners and losers. They advocated for the kingdom Jesus spoke of, a kingdom in which friend and enemy alike are honored, valued, and accepted. Victory is defined as turning the heart of one's enemy until goodness prevails for all, a much more difficult strategy than merely overthrowing one's enemy.

The Kingdom of God

In his role as anti-messiah, Jesus continually came back to a central theme, "the kingdom of God." The sheer number of times he used the term and the centrality it played in his messages make it a primary interpretive lens through which we understand his teaching.

He summed up the kingdom when he taught the disciples to pray that things on earth would be as they are in heaven.[34] In all Jesus's interactions this was his objective, to make things on earth as they are in the heart of God. When he was interacting with the diseased of body and soul, smug Pharisees, obstinate Romans, guilt-ridden tax collectors, or collaborating stewards, Jesus was always working toward the same objective: God's kingdom on earth. When the objective is the manifestation of divine goodness

---

34. Matt 6:10.

on earth, violence, retribution, arm twisting, or put-on holiness just doesn't work. They're not the kinds of strategies that effectively introduce the heart of God on the earth.

To the Zealots, tax collectors and stewards were traitors. They symbolized everything wrong with Israel. If anyone was deserving of messianic wrath it was them. But Jesus turned the expectations of the Zealots on their heads in the way he dealt with tax collectors. Rather than rebuking them, he awakened their slumbering spiritual sensibilities. He treated them with respect and favor, healing the burden of guilt and shame under which they labored. He called them back to the divine truth that would set them free, and invited them back into the family of God. This was not the messiah the Zealots were looking for.[35]

To the Pharisees, sinners were the cause of Israel's suffering. They were inviting God's wrath on the entire nation, the root cause of national humiliation and suffering. If anyone was deserving of messianic wrath, it was them. But Jesus disappointed their expectations as well. Jesus was a friend to sinners. To sinners bearing the shame of failure and exposure, Jesus offered healing, forgiveness, and an invitation back into community. His was a strategy of healing, truth, mercy, and forgiveness. His strategy was to bring the divine nature to bear on earth, to make things on earth as they are in heaven. This was not the messiah the Pharisees were looking for.

To Roman soldiers, Jesus ministered truth that set them free. To those with blinded souls, Jesus offered sight. To those with authentic questions, Jesus sat through the night answering. To the crowds, Jesus taught grace and goodness and connection to the divine Spirit. This was a different kind of messiah than everybody was expecting. This was a different kind of kingdom than anyone was expecting.

Following Jesus the Man

We no longer live in a Newtonian world. Quantum physicists have given us a new reality. Now that time bends and light can be both wave and particle, paradox works; the paradoxical parts of our faith work. History is giving us a chance to correct the blindness of our Enlightenment past. Enlightenment Christianity could only pay attention to one dimension of Jesus's nature.

35. Luke 19.

Seeing with new eyes, we can pursue the wisdom and truth that exist in both the divinity *and* the humanity of Jesus. We can equally follow the divine *and* the human Jesus.

For Jesus the man, salvation wasn't about a good afterlife, it was about being saved from Roman oppression, from domination, injustice, and exploitation. Deeper still, salvation was from the internal ravages of evil, from dishonesty, fear, mean-spiritedness, and small-heartedness. Jesus focused on connecting people to the inner life of God, saving us from the soul forces that fracture relationships, fracture personalities, and fracture our destinies.

Jesus the man lived in *this* world, cared about *this* world, and sought to bring God's rule to *this* world.

To fully follow Jesus, how can we do anything else?

This is our religion.

It is just as important to help people eat as it is to point them to paradise. If we follow Jesus the fully human man, we'll care just as much about justice as we do about evangelism. It is the fullness of our faith to resist injustice, fight for fairness, contend for dignity, and make sure everybody gets equal access to resource. It is our mission as Jesus's followers to work for a world where justice flows down like waters and righteousness like a mighty stream.[36]

Followers of Jesus care about people's bodies, about their schools, about their planet, and about inequities in health care, education, and opportunity. Followers of Jesus care that some people have access to nutritional food and others do not. It is the spirituality of Jesus to make right what is wrong on the earth, and to make fair what is unjust on the earth.

When we follow Jesus, these instincts get embedded in our spiritual DNA. It becomes natural for us to rearrange our lives this way. We drop lesser priorities and activities and free up bandwidth for the work of bettering the earth.

We resist injustice when we see it. We don't enjoy the profit, prosperity, and blessing of unjust systems. Rather, we notice when others go without, when others suffer. As Americans who follow Jesus, we become more sensitized to the injustices our economic system imposes on other nations. We become keenly aware of how costly our access to inexpensive goods and services is

36. Amos 5:24.

to other peoples. Ours cannot be the posture of the Herodian, simply going along with the system because it works for us.

When we follow the human Jesus, ours are lives of justice and compassion. Our perspective expands; we see how social, economic, and political systems skew fairness and then we go to work setting things right. When we gain a favored or advantaged position in life, we look around for those who suffer, and extend favor and advantage to them. We do unto others what we would have them do unto us. If we were stuck in a cycle of alienation, poverty, or psycho-emotional woundedness we would want someone to come for us. If we were stuck in a bad place and blinded to the way out we would want someone to come for us.

Following Jesus the man is a tall order. Making things on earth as they are in heaven is a lofty and demanding agenda. Going for the long win rather than the quick and easy one makes for a challenging life. Contending for everybody to win, rather than just me and my people is an arduous proposition.

As followers of Jesus, *this* is our religion.

Rethinking What Happened

10

Restoring Mystery to Easter

The Devolution of Purgatory: A Cautionary Tale

The vitality of Christian communities fades over time. It happens to churches, it happens to denominations, and it happens to movements, again and again through history. This cycle of ebb and flow usually mirrors some kind of corrosion in our community's story.

Imagine a group of saints in the early years of our faith. Imagine them living devoutly, spiritually, and bearing the fruit of virtue and goodness. Then imagine what they must have been thinking as they saw their deaths approaching. Their faith told them that after death they would experience mysterious union with God. But as mature as they had become, they were painfully aware of how unready they were to join in oneness with God. Like brides not quite ready for their weddings, they saw in themselves residual pride, greed, envy, and other weaknesses. How could it be, they wondered, that they would be joined with the eternal Divine while still carrying these base elements within themselves?

Speculating about their afterlives, about how they would move from their current state into full union with God, I imagine them feeling the same discomfort I do when I contemplate my own union with God. "There must be a purging process to remove these vestiges of illusion and shortcoming," they might have thought. "I don't know how it will happen, but there must be a purging of my soul that prepares me for union with the Divine. Yes, that's what awaits me: a preparatory purging."

And with a sense of hope and promise they laid their heads down to die, carrying in their hearts an abiding sense of peace, assurance, and confidence in the goodness of God.

And after they died their children became the keepers of the story. Picking up where their parents left off, they refined it just a bit. "A purging. Yes. That's what it must be." And as people do, they made the story a little more understandable, adding some real estate and a clock. Now the purging happened in a place and at a time. "When we die," they said, "we go to a place and stay there while the purging process takes place. When we're finally ready for mystic union with God we leave that place and off we go." They called the place "purgatory," the place of purging.

And with a sense of anticipation, and hope, they laid down their heads and died. And their children took up the story.

"Purgatory, yes!" they said. "And you know what? Uncle Louie died a while ago, and he was surely *not* ready for union with God, being the rascal he was. He must still be in purgatory. You know what? We should pray for him to move on to union with God. I bet our prayers would help him move on to whatever awaits him."

And with a little less peace, and hoping that their own kids would pray for them when they were in purgatory, they laid down their heads and died. And their children took up the story.

"It is good that we are all praying for our Uncle Louies," they said, "but some of us have become lax in our prayers. That's just not right! Let's see what we can do to motivate each other. We need a little guilt to motivate, and some candles to remind us. Yes, that should help."

And with a little guilt and fatigue, and just a shade of fear, they laid down their heads and died. And their children took up the story.

"You know . . . these candles are costing us a fortune! We're missing a trick here. We should make prayers for our departed loved ones a *privilege*. If we did that, we could kill two birds with one stone. First, we would motivate people to pray, and second, we'd make a tidy sum.

"Let's do this. Let's hold a few special prayer services for dead celebrities. That way, everybody will want a special service. With that kind of demand, we can charge people. That way we'll get people praying for their relatives *and* we'll make money! People will get the message that the more you pay the better the service, the better the candles, and the quicker your loved ones will get out of purgatory. So, cough up! You love your family, don't you? You're a good son or daughter, aren't you?"

Each successive generation took only a small step from the previous one. Each step was taken with good intent (except maybe that last one). Each generation made the story just a little more practical, a little more understandable, and a little bit better. But for all their good intent, through the generations, a truth that inspired hope and peace devolved into a fear-inducing, wearying narrative of guilt, shame, and obligation.

That's what happens to stories over time.

And so, we ought always to be wondering about how *we're* telling our story. We ought always to be vigilant lest *we* be the generation that encrusts it by making things just a bit more practical, understandable, and logical.

In this section we'll see this is exactly what has happened to our Christian story of sin and salvation. The devolutionary process that happens over time has distorted it. We'll end this section by going back in our history to see some of the ways our ancient forebears spoke of salvation before the distortion.

Death to Ambiguity!

If we're going to rethink our salvation story, we ought to start at the beginning, with Easter. Easter is troubling. It always has been. Paul himself called it foolishness and a stumbling block.[1] Nevertheless, generation after generation, it remains the centerpiece of our faith.

Even so, the way we talk about Easter has accumulated baggage through the years. For many in the quantum era it has lost its vitality. However, because of its revered status it often feels disconcerting to rethink such sacred ground.

When an idea is difficult, it is a natural instinct to try to make it easier. That's what we've done with Easter. The story of Jesus's death and resurrection we tell today has evolved over centuries of "fixing." Each generation has tried to tell the story to its children in a way that makes just a little more sense.

1. 1 Cor 1:23.

Although well-intentioned, this has resulted in a story with almost all of the mystery squeezed out of it. A concrete story always makes more sense to children and feels much better than a vague, mysterious, ambiguous one.

As each generation has tried to make Easter more understandable, we've tended to gloss over the blurry or bewildering parts. That tendency notwithstanding, the earliest accounts of Easter are confusing, jumbled, messy, and untidy. The early authors seemed to struggle for words to convey something they didn't quite have a handle on. To the careful reader, it feels like these people, even decades later when they wrote things down, were trying to talk about something they didn't fully understand.

Before Easter, Jesus was confusing enough. He said things people couldn't understand. He did things they hadn't seen before, but at least he existed in the same reality they did. He got around like normal people got around. He walked places, rode donkeys, and sailed in boats. But after Easter, he just *appeared* places. He started just *being there*.

Jesus after Easter was different from Jesus before Easter. After Easter, people who had known him didn't recognize him. Mary didn't recognize him in the garden. Disciples on the road to Emmaus didn't recognize him. His friends in a boat didn't recognize him on the beach. Only after adjusting to a new kind of reality, after reflecting on experiences they couldn't comprehend, did they realize that in some way they had experienced Jesus.

Jesus after Easter was different from Jesus before Easter.

Scholars quibble about when each book of the Christian scriptures was written, but everybody agrees that Paul wrote his letters long before the gospel accounts. In Galatians, one of our earliest Christian scriptures, Paul wrote of "seeing" Jesus. It's clear from the context, however, that he didn't see Jesus the way people saw him before Easter. It wasn't a flesh-and-bones kind of seeing. "It pleased God to reveal Jesus in me," is the way he wrote it.[2] How vague is that? Yet he made no distinction between his encounter with the risen Jesus and the encounters of the disciples who experienced him in Jerusalem. In fact, when he needed to defend his apostleship with the Corinthian church he cited his encounter with Jesus as evidence that he was on the same footing as the original apostles.[3]

2. Gal 1:13–17.
3. 1 Cor 9:1, 15:8–9.

After Easter, scripture recounts two ways people "saw" Jesus. One was fuzzy and mysterious, the other concrete and specific. It is interesting that the earlier accounts are the fuzzier ones. Later, as the story was told and retold, the accounts became a little more pinned down, a little more concrete. Today when we tell the story of Easter, we tend to eliminate all the ambiguous, mysterious accounts. The after-Easter Jesus is clear and understandable. Ours is a coherent and very imaginable account. Jesus's body, once dead, is now resuscitated. He was dead. His heart stopped beating. His brain waves stopped waving. Then on the third day a miracle happened and his heart started beating again. He stretched his arms, took off the burial clothes, got up, and walked out of the grave.

When we depict Easter in movies that's the way we show it. Through the years, we've reduced the story's troubling parts down to one really big miracle: dead becomes alive. Everything else in the story is sanitized, normalized, and comprehensible. Easter has become unambiguous. We even created a doctrine to make sure it stays that way. We call it the "literal, physical, resurrection" doctrine and some insist we all assent to this doctrine if we want to be Christian.

In the Enlightenment era, giving ourselves to this reductionist process made Easter very reasonable. If we could swallow one really big miracle, the rest fit easily into our minds. There was much less equivocation and only a little bit of mystery. We liked it that way. Once we got over the dead-becomes-alive part, the rest made perfect sense.

But now we live in the quantum era. Now all the clarity we worked into our story makes it sound hollow and empty. When our universe becomes ambiguous and paradoxical, a sanitized story is less engaging.

Easter didn't begin in this sanitized form. It began with a lot more vagueness, a lot more uncertainty. It began with more possibility, more breadth, freedom, space, and scope. It began with less restriction and was a whole lot less locked down.

It was a story the quantum era could hear.

Putting Mystery Back in Our Easter Story

I imagine that the accounts of Jesus after Easter are confusing because the people who experienced Jesus were confused. I imagine Easter so bewildered people that they struggled for words to talk about it. Instead of telling one another exactly what happened, I imagine them saying that *something* happened, something that changed everything for everyone. But for all their efforts to put words on it, it was an event that couldn't be pinned down to a cohesive report. I imagine an Easter so shrouded in mystery, so straining of mental concepts, that those who went through it couldn't stitch together an adequate tale to tell.

And now, it is to our generation to restore Easter to its previous, ambiguous glory. It is to us to restore all the beautiful vagueness it used to have. I'm telling my own children and the children in our community an Easter story about people who experienced God so profoundly they couldn't even be coherent. I go on to tell them that the experience of those long ago invites us to seek our own profound, personal, and intimate experiences of the spirit of the risen Jesus.

The scriptural accounts of those who experienced the risen Jesus are accounts of surprise and disorientation. The same has been true through the generations. Being surprised by the divine is part of our heritage. When we take the ambiguity out of Easter, we do make it feel just a little less scandalous for our children, but we also leave little room for surprise. When we normalize Easter and make it easier, more logical, and more accessible, despite all our good intentions, we diminish our spiritual lives.

As we've said, people tend to find what they look for. If our story tells us to look for surprise, we often find surprise. If our story speaks of an experience bigger than can be contained, that is what we look for, and that is what we find. In each generation Christians have reported profound and disorienting experiences of the risen spirit of Jesus invading their souls and shaking their reality deeply.

That's how Easter began, as a jumbled, confused explosion of divine drama that didn't lend itself to practical, coherent storytelling. It especially did not lend itself to systematic doctrinal assertions. It was a story rooted in experience and shrouded in the unknown. This is how it began, and this is how we ought to give it to our children. As mystery makes a comeback in the quantum reality, reality is weirder than we thought. It is more inconclusive and uncertain than we thought. In this world, it no longer works to reduce things to the reasonable or the expected. We need to go back to our unpolished story, our surprising, scandalous, imprecise, and mysterious story.

Easter changed the lives of those who experienced it. It forever unwound their hearts and minds. It transformed their expectations about the way things are and changed them forever.

When we keep our story vague, it invites us to be watchful and alert for this same kind of mysterious, transformative wonder. Those who went before us point us to the *experience* of Easter, not a belief about it. Experience changes us. As we'll see in the next chapter, reality categories are broken for those who experience the risen Jesus. Something happens to us in the experience. And those who attempt to describe the experience struggle. They use images like leaving darkness and entering the light. They speak of overcoming death and being set free from prison. But these are *experiential* words. They invite us into surprise, into transformation, and into a new dimension of life.

The Enlightenment Easter story focused on clarifying exactly what happened to Jesus's body. It focused on making sure everything was clear and that we all believed the same thing. A quantum Easter can focus on *experiencing* it. It can invite us back to surprise and transformation. Our rethought narrative can be once again unbound and untidy. If we give our children *this* Easter, we invite them to personal encounters with divine mystery that are as wide and diverse as those of other generations before us.

He Is Risen. He is Risen Indeed!

> You became believers because you trusted . . . that Christ is alive, risen from the dead. If there's no resurrection, there's no living Christ. And face it—if there's no resurrection for Christ, everything we've told you is smoke and mirrors, and everything you've staked your life on is smoke and mirrors. Not only that, but we are guilty of telling a string of barefaced lies about God, all these affidavits we passed on to you verifying that God raised up Christ— sheer fabrications . . . if there's no resurrection.[4]

4. 1 Cor 15:12–19.

The experience of Easter is central to our faith. For hundreds of years we have greeted one another on Easter morning with the same words: "He is risen," and the reply, "He is risen, indeed." Our greeting affirms what happened to those living long ago, who saw Jesus die, who experienced him defeating death, and who subsequently lived a new kind of life. In our greeting we affirm that death does not have the power we thought it did. We affirm that life triumphs over death.

It is a greeting that speaks of wild, unnatural, riotous experience. It calls us to breath-stopping, scandalous shock. Jesus, it tells us, rendered our reality categories moot. It is not merely assent to an event we all agree happened. In our words, we awaken the anticipation that each of us can experience the new life Jesus showed us.

When our ancestors experienced the un-dead Jesus it changed everything for them. Though words could not contain their experience, words were all they had. Their words point us to an experience of our own.

For them, the un-dead Jesus was real in one way. He ate fish.[5] That was one category of "real" in their minds. However, he also transcended "real," existing in a way that bridged the physical and the spiritual, the real and the *bigger-than-real*.

Casting about for words, they spoke of the perishable being clothed in the imperishable, the mortal taking on immortality. Death, they said, could be swallowed up by life, its power stolen away.[6] Trying to tease out mysteries beyond comprehension, they spoke of boundless and vast experience. The way Jesus was revealed to them was beyond anything they had considered.

They used the metaphor of a seed being sown into the ground. It looked dead, but out of deadness a new kind of life was born. It went into the ground one way; it came out another way. Like the seed, life goes into the ground as a physical body, but gets raised as something entirely different.

And that's not all! This wild thing that happened to Jesus, they told one another, is only the beginning! Jesus was only the first to experience this perishable-imperishable mystery. Whatever it was that happened to him will happen again and again and again, to us!

5. Luke 24:42.
6. 1 Cor 15:53–55.

They spoke of a brand new category of reality, an existence in which death was not death, but merely a new way of being. We wouldn't die as we previously thought. Rather, we would be changed, changed the way Jesus was changed. In a flash, in the twinkling of an eye, deadness was transformed into some kind of an imperishable reality.

These were categories never imagined before. Jesus after Easter awakened us to a different universe, a universe progressing toward divine hope and promise.[7] Those who experienced Jesus after Easter glimpsed a future in which all people, all creation, once pronounced "good" by God, could once again shine in their truest forms. Their experience filled them with hope for redemption and restoration. They began to see themselves caught up in a cosmic adventure in which all the universe, the rocks, the trees, and the people, were groaning with the pangs of birth, preparing for a destiny and future of life and hope.

It was an experience too big for words.

This is the kind of story we want to give our children. It is big enough to reconfigure our lives. It changes the meaning of our final breath, and every breath before that one. It is a story that awakens expectations beyond expectations.

It is a story that is big enough to change us. It is a story worthy of giving our children.

A Story Big Enough to Change Us

Rethinking our Easter story can change us. It can invite us into a dimension of divine experience that transforms us. In our religion's history, when people encounter the Divine personally this is exactly what happens. We become conduits of divine Life on the earth. Historically, people who experience the risen Jesus are people who love. They love the poor. They draw from a deep inner reserve. They heal the wounded and raise up those beaten down by life. It happened a lot in the first three hundred years of our religion. In those years we revolutionized the known world with love. A good story invites us into the depth of spiritual experience that does that. Getting our doctrine right, not so much.

7. Rom 8:19–21.

In our Easter story, our ancestors glimpsed life beyond life and experienced unlimited divine love. They were not afraid of death. They were not afraid of God. And not fearing for their own lives, they related to the world differently. Setting their eyes on the unseen they didn't fear being crucified, crushed, tortured, or destroyed. Theirs was an imperishable future.

Enflamed by a glimpse of mystery bigger than they could explain, they carried in their hearts a message of hope, love, goodness, and forgiveness. They went out with a message of good news. They served people. They loved people. They cared for those crushed under Roman aggression. They loved their enemies and prayed for their persecutors. They laid down a path for generations to follow, transforming their own generation, and history.

And then they grew old.

And they began to die. But having seen in Jesus what they saw, they were marked forever. Theirs was an unquenchable hope in the face of death. They laid their heads down with an unflappable peace. They laid down their laurels of compassion, kindness, and goodness. They died ignited with hope, confident that Jesus was the firstborn of many. With their last breaths they looked toward the mysterious future life Jesus had demonstrated. "Believe me," he had said, "you will never die!"[8]

And so, on Roman gallows or in the throes of old age, they faced death with their eyes fixed on a bright horizon. Their experience of Jesus after Easter, their brush with the transcendent, gave them a deep assurance that the day they died was the day they graduated into a new and mysterious dimension of life.

And their story is our story.

It is a story about uncontainable experience, not containable doctrine.

Reducing Easter to a doctrine about what happened to Jesus's body diminishes our tradition, our experience, and the wild, unlimited experience of our faith.

A story about awakening to reality beyond reality inspires us to look for, and find, the Spirit of God within us, around us, and flowing through us to the world we live in.

8. John 11:26.

A few years ago as Easter approached, I was reading a bunch of sermons by other ministers. I ran across a story told by a minister in Seattle that I deeply appreciated. He told about his mother's death in a way that spoke to reality beyond reality, bigger than life and overwhelming expectations.

> I will never forget my last conversation with my mom. She died not that long ago, and it is still tough. She told me she didn't want to die because she just purchased new blue carpet for the new apartment. She had the same beige carpet for twenty years in her old, low income apartment and the carpet was beige brown. They put in brand new blue carpet in her brand new apartment. The new apartment had a view of the cornfields of Minnesota. She said, "I don't want to die. I really like the new carpet. I have a nice apartment and it has a view of the cornfields."

And she died.

> Oh, poor mother. Poor us. In the new reality, I bet Mom said, "This is better than blue carpet! This is better than cornfields in Minnesota. I bet Mom was astonished and astounded, amazed and awestruck, dazzled and dumbfounded by the beauty that was beyond her imagination.[9]

Ours is a story that points us to reality beyond reality. It points us to a way that is bigger than the limited way most live. It points us to truth beyond the truth we swim in every day. It points us to life beyond life.

Easter points us to experience, the experience of higher life. That changes us. It changes everything. It inspires in us a love that is bigger than the reduced version we settle for. It insists on more grace than we know how to accept. It speaks of divine Presence we don't typically look for. It motivates us to seek out and dance with the inner Divine that is always present, always here, always now.

And that's just the bigger-than-this-life part of our story.

Wait until we talk about the transcending-our-two-natures part.

9. Markquart, "Astonished," para. 19.

11

The Harsh Side of Our Story

The Christian Story and the Human Dilemma

We all resonate with Paul when he complains about what it feels like to be human. "I can't understand myself," he grumbles. "The things I hate are the things I do. The things I want to do, I don't end up doing. It's a pickle! How do I get out of it?"[1]

Yep. That's what it's like to be human.

Ours is a beautiful story. It awakens us to our divine-image glory, but it doesn't discount the lesser nature with which we must daily cope. It takes an unvarnished look at the dilemma of being human but climaxes with crashing crescendo offering us a powerful way out. It points us to a profound solution to the universal struggle Paul articulated so well. "*This* is how you get out the pickle, Paul!"

Our story begins in a garden of purity, innocence, and goodness. It is an auspicious beginning. The life of God is breathed into our souls, animating us with divine life and infusing us with a beautiful, pure, and blameless nature. But like all good stories, conflict spoils the idyllic setting. Here comes a serpent, a temptation, a rebellion, and deep knowledge of evil. It is a narrative that helps us make meaning of our experience. Each of us can find ourselves in the story. Consequently, it helps us think about our own souls: how they are divided between two loyalties, how they are torn between fidelity to our

---

1. Rom 7:15.

divine image and to our more base, often wicked nature. It affirms our divine image, but it also warns us we need to address our more nefarious instincts.

It also helps us understand one another. It helps us imagine the first human generation, all subsequent generations, and our own. We *all* face this struggle. We are *all* caught in the predicament; we *all* suffer the dilemma.

Ours is a beautiful story.

It describes the human quandary, the pickle, but it doesn't stop there. As it unfolds through our scriptures, it also shows us a way out, a path by which we can move beyond our divided loyalties. It tells us that the divine life in us can be restored to its former prominence, and that we can move from darkness to light, wickedness to goodness. In Jesus we are offered a lifeline to pull us out of our predicament. Generation after generation, those who experience the story's promise of new life speak of being "saved," "redeemed," "restored," and "made whole."

But as we've seen, beautiful stories become encrusted stories. All it takes is time.

An Unvarnished Telling

In many ways our story has turned ugly through the years.

One of the joys of childhood is our youthful ability to suspend critical analysis for the joy of a good story. When we were children, pointing out a story's problems was just not important. Rather, our joy was to embrace the tale eagerly, to enjoy it for its own sake, and savor how each detail unfolded along the way. Many Christians absorbed our story of sin and salvation when we were children. Consequently, we haven't always faced up to the narrative's troublesome parts.

But consider this bald, unvarnished way of telling our story.

God is omnipotent and omniscient, all-powerful and all-knowing. This means that he made the whole universe, everything in it, and knew how the whole thing would turn out. Being all-powerful, God was not bound by the rules of the universe, but *made* the rules of the universe. He set the whole thing up, including the rules of human nature. He made the whole thing up. It is his game.

It was God who made human beings with the ability and disposition to sin (that's the all-powerful part). God made human beings knowing full well that they *would* sin (that's the all-knowing part). Then, once we *did* sin, God turned his back on us, saddled us with a debt we couldn't pay, and levied us with the stiffest of punishments, eternal torment. We sinful human beings must pay the ultimate penalty of death and separation from God (hell) for a crime no worse than being who God made us to be, for doing what God knew we would do. Furthermore, his rules say, there is not a thing we can ever do about it.

God made up a rule that says anybody who sins is condemned to die. This is not just a physical death followed by nonexistence. No. This is *spiritual* death, *eternal* death, death we call separation from God. It is a death that hurts. It is a death that never stops hurting. The hurt goes on and on and on. Forever.

Further, because of the sin of the first generation of people on the planet, every subsequent man, woman, and child inherits a badness-gene that ensures they will sin, too. So everybody has to pay. Nobody escapes. Everybody who doesn't figure out how to pay the debt that can't be paid must be punished.

In this telling, God is so pure and perfect that he cannot abide to be in the presence of sin. Consequently, he cannot abide us. We are sinful. Our sin, and the sin of Adam and Eve, has earned us God's rejection and alienation. Our bed has been made for us and now we have to lie in it. The infection of sin is in all of us, so we all have to pay the piper.

That's the bad news in this version of the story, but there is some good news.

Showing his gracious and merciful side, God visited earth. He poured his nature into a perfect human being: Jesus. To help us out of the jam we were in, God vested his own nature in an innocent man. Then, to make things right, God had Jesus beaten up, flogged, and crucified. He insisted Jesus suffer for everybody else's sin and then turned his face away from him (because he couldn't abide sin), and he rejected the perfect man for the sin he carried.

And once it was all over, once the innocent man had suffered the wages of sin, once innocent blood had been shed on behalf of the guilty, God's wrath over the whole affair was sufficiently satisfied. Once blood sacrifice had been paid, God's honor was sufficiently restored, and he allowed humanity back into his good graces.

This is admittedly a harsh way of telling the story. Few Christians would tell it that harshly. Most often when it is told, we focus on the importance of free will. For love to be love, human beings must be free agents. This requires free will, which, unfortunately, ends badly. It is free will that creates sin and suffering. There are usually words about God voluntarily limiting his power to grant us the freedom to choose. In God's quest for our love, he has to honor our bad choices.

When the story is usually told, there is a great deal more nuance than in the unvarnished version above. However, when the spin is stripped away, we can't get around it: the basic plotline is a harsh one. God creates most human beings knowing that they won't get things right, won't find the right hoop to jump through, or won't pray the right salvation prayer. He creates most human beings knowing that theirs will be a horrific ending.

This basic story line can't get away from the omnipotence and omniscience of God. Knowing things would be this way, God made things this way.

It's hard to stomach. It seems unfair. It paints God in a capricious, unjust, and unsporting light. All in all, it's a pretty dirty business and God is at the center of it.

And so, a lot of people these days aren't distracted by the spin anymore, and are giving the Christian God a wide berth. If any person we knew treated a dog like that, let alone their own son, well, that's just somebody we would avoid. How is it we should feel so indebted to a God who made such a dirty, unjust, unrighteous system? How is it we should love, with all our heart, soul, mind, and strength, this God who created such crummy rules? "Well, no thank you," most people are saying. "You stay over there; I'll stay over here."

This stripped-down telling of our Enlightenment story should give Christians pause as well.

If it were not so common, so mainstream, we'd be repulsed by it. If so many hadn't heard it when we were kids, when it was natural to suspend critical analysis, we would despise it. Its fundamental implications are that God is *not* eternally loving, that God made us one way and then rejected us for being that way, and that God despises what he created.

As common and venerated as this telling of our sin-salvation story is, it needs some rethinking.

Anselm and Niagara

When Christians tell this story, most assume it is the one and true way to tell it. Most believe this is the standard, orthodox, and approved account of sin and salvation.

But it is not.

It is a version that gained traction relatively late in our history. It is one among several ways of talking about sin and salvation. It draws from a few scriptures but ignores others, draws from the writings of a few in our tradition, but ignores others.

In the eleventh century, a theologian named Anselm was trying to tell our sin-salvation story in a way that made sense to his generation.[2] His was a world of medieval politics and economics. Feudal hierarchy was the order of his day. Drawing from metaphors at hand to make sense of salvation, he spoke of God's honor being offended by sin. He spoke of divine honor that had to be restored. That's the way things worked in the medieval world. Political, economic, and social order were held together by a hierarchy of lords and vassals. Honor, faithfulness, and fidelity were the glue that held society together.

It was a great metaphor for the time and Anselm worked it hard. He suggested that God played the role of the feudal lord, and we his vassals. The problem with sin was that it broke the honor code between lord and vassal. The infidelity of a broken oath was more than a personal affront. It broke the system that held society together. Once sin was cast as a broken feudal oath, it was seen as breaking the order of the world. No matter how God felt about sin personally, the fundamental stability of the universe had to be set right.

Before the rule of law, everyone understood how a vassal's disobedience undercut social structure. It just made sense to Anselm's generation that sin broke the cosmic order. They also understood that a broken universe required a radical remedy. Dramatic redress was required. The penalty for

2. Hood, "The Cross," 282–83.

a vassal breaking his fealty oath to the lord was death, so it just made sense that Jesus's death was payment for sinful humanity breaking the world.

In Anselm's narrative the lord's honor didn't have to be restored so he would feel better. Honor was not that trivial. It was much more important than the feelings of a single individual. The lord's honor had to be restored because it was the foundation of the whole social, political, and economic system. A broken covenant ripped the social fabric, inviting chaos and anarchy. Consequently, sin, to Anselm, violated God's honor and stood as an unanswered rupture of everything that exists. It had to be made right to keep the universe functioning. Sin could not simply be forgiven willy-nilly. Something profound had to happen to preserve God's honor and dignity lest everything fall apart. God was bound to exact payment for sin. The whole system's integrity depended on restoring God's honor and dignity.

With this framework running in his mind, Anselm scoured the scriptures to explain things. He deeply resonated with those scriptures that speak of Jesus's death as a sacrificial payment. For him, Jesus's death satisfied God's dignity, restored God's honor, and repaired the breach in the universe. His version of the story made perfect sense to those living in feudal times. It matched their world and fit the way things worked. It had a comforting familiarity that touched their hearts deeply.

And it stuck—long after feudalism was gone.

Then in the late 1800s, this way of telling our story got another boost. It was a worrying time for Christians. Darwin had explained human origins in terms that made many uncomfortable. Theologians were studying biblical criticism. They were discovering things about the Bible that made folks even more uncomfortable. The rising tide of scientific modernism felt like an attack. Stable ground was eroding under Christian feet and many began to look for solid footing. Some began to cast about for a set of fundamental beliefs to hold on to. There was a need for comfort, for security, and for beliefs that felt firm, trustworthy, and unyielding.

That's when the Bible Conference we mentioned in chapter one started gaining traction.

Each summer near Niagara, New York, attendees gathered to talk about the essential, unshakable fundamentals one needed to retain to be Christian. In 1878 they issued a document outlining a set of indispensable, indisputable, requisite doctrines. Ignoring several other historical versions of the sin-salvation story, they chose Anselm's version to be one of their fourteen non-negotiables.[3] If you were going to be a Christian, they said, you had to believe Anselm's salvation story. They called it the "penal-substitution theory of the atonement." The focus of this version is that Jesus bore the *penalty* for sin, and his death *substituted* for everybody else's.

As our history has unfolded, this sin-salvation story has become *the* official version for many Christians. Jesus, following the model of the Old Testament system of animal sacrifice, functioned as the Lamb of God, a substitutionary blood offering on behalf of the sin of others, gaining God's forgiveness for all who accept it.

Despite its prominent place in our faith, there is a toxic and hurtful side to the Anselm-Niagara story.

Richard Rohr tells of a bumper sticker his New Mexico community created. It said, "God does not love you because you are good. You are good because God loves you." They sat on that idea for a while, but later decided to update it. "God does not love you because you are good. God loves you because God is good."[4]

Those simple words move us. They ring deeply of truth and resonate within us. However, they do *not* resonate with an unvarnished telling of the Anselm-Niagara story. If we deeply embrace the goodness of God, it challenges this way of thinking about sin and salvation. Those who learned the Anselm-Niagara story as the only way to talk about salvation find it difficult to consider anything else. Any alternative challenges the script believed to be the one and true truth. Even with underlying toxicity, once a story gets normalized in our hearts and minds, it is difficult to trade it in for a new one.

That's a problem.

Arguing Torah

When my son was a sophomore in college, he would often call me after his comparative religion class. At first, I think he was trying to shock his minister dad with his newfound religious discoveries. When he found me

3. Saxon, "Interacting," 4.
4. Rohr, *Things Hidden*, 164.

unshocked he might have been a bit disappointed, but over the semester, our between-class chats were warm and interesting discussions on the meaning of religion. I recall one chat after a class in which he had learned about the Jewish tradition of "arguing Torah."

My son is a peacemaker at heart. Since he was a child, when anybody argued at home, it made him visibly uncomfortable. When he learned that Judaism revered argument as a spiritual discipline it didn't sit well with him. Aside from his personal discomfort with conflict, it was unsettling that religion in general had enough wiggle room, enough ambiguity, to sustain centuries of argument.

"It seems," he said, "that if religion were true, after a while, we'd have found the truth, and there wouldn't be anything left to argue about. If religion were true," he thought out loud, "it wouldn't be open for interpretation by every Tom, Dick, and Harry with an opinion."

"I wish I could give you a religion of certainty," I told him, "but this life we woke up in just isn't that way. Our experience of God isn't constant. It morphs and changes through our lives and through the generations. The way we think about God today is very different from the way people thought about God in the past. Throughout history, we continually outgrow our old understandings of God, and replace them with new ones."

I went on to describe two beautiful things embedded in the Jewish tradition of arguing Torah. First, I told him, their religion started before our Western love affair with certitude. With ambiguity in their DNA, their commitment to community is deeper than their commitment to certainty. They'll argue passionately today, and still be together tomorrow. Our Protestant tradition, on the other hand, started *during* the era of certitude seeking. Consequently, when *we* argue religion, we assume only one of us can be right. Tragically, it has been our way to simply break relationship when we hit an impasse. We tend to abandon community and form another sect of Protestantism. The Jewish way is better.

The second thing so beautiful about arguing Torah, I told him, is how well it works with the premise that the deepest spiritual things cannot be fully contained in human understanding. Transcendence is too big to fit in our hearts or brains. By arguing with one another we continually unearth higher and deeper ways of thinking about and experiencing God. We never fully arrive. God is too big for that. But by arguing together, our understanding keeps moving forward. We make space for dynamic, always-morphing, always-changing, and always-evolving insight. Jewish people have an elastic view of God that allows them to keep drawing closer to the Divine, generation after generation. We, on the other hand, often get stuck in a static, once-for-always understanding of God.

We could really afford to argue our story a bit these days. Things in our churches are going badly. People who study us tell us that our collective morality, ethics, and spiritual health aren't going well for us.[5] Our framing narrative *needs* some reworking. Fewer and fewer of us live lives of deep and abiding virtue. Our reputation in the world drops a bit further each year. The ways we live, do business, practice our sexuality, and relate to others are often hypocritical, selfish, and judgmental. Again, we could afford to take a fresh look at the story we're living.

So let's do what our Jewish cousins do. Let's argue a bit, try out new ideas and new ways of telling our story. Breaking eggs is our generation's job. That's how omelets get made. Let's break some eggs together.

---

5. Barna, *Second Coming*, 1–15.

12

Problems with the Anselm-Niagara Story

Because the Anselm-Niagara story is so venerated it is difficult to talk about it as one salvation narrative among many. Many Christians grew up thinking it was the only way to talk about "being saved." Like any metaphor pressed too far, it breaks down on several points. However, it has held such a prominent place for so long that any attempt to rethink it feels disloyal. To help us in our rethinking endeavor, let's look a bit more closely at some of the problems inherent in Anselm-Niagara.

Problem 1: A Mean, Capricious God

Most problematic about the Anselm-Niagara story is the assumption on which it rests. It makes it difficult to think of God as good in any sense of the word we understand. It makes God punitive at best—capricious, angry, and bloodthirsty at worst. If nothing else, it conjures images of God that are quite unapproachable.

Every Christian knows the party line. God is love. Anselm-Niagara, however, undercuts the party line.

This story implies God has a mean streak. He creates rules for the universe by which some will never win. He stacks the rules against a lot of people. Under Anselm-Niagara, most will end their existence suffering eternal torment. That's just the way it goes. It was acceptable in God's thinking to go ahead and create humanity knowing things would turn out this way. So there's some collateral damage, oh well.

For all our talk about God's goodness, wrath and damnation are the subtext here. The Anselm-Niagara story maintains that in the fullness of time, the day will come when God's true, angry nature will finally be set loose. It tells us, "You'll be sorry then, buddy! God will destroy the world and condemn all those who didn't get their religion right."

Problem 2: An Anthropomorphic God

Another troubling element of Anselm-Niagara is how it reduces our image of God. In it, God looks and acts just like a human being. God's instincts, feelings, and responses mirror those of the human heart. He vacillates between grace and vengeance just like humans do. He is noble and generous on one hand, but when pressed too far, he vents all the same anger and vengeance we do. Anthropomorphism is lurking just under the surface.

As we said earlier, human metaphors for God are often helpful on the spiritual journey. However, when we limit metaphors to human ones, we suffer the blind spots of our reduction. If God *were* like a human, then of course he *would* act the way he does in Anselm-Niagara. Sure, he would get fed up with sin. That's what humans do. Certainly, he would break relationship and punish people when they violate his rules of goodness. That's what humans do. It happens all the time.

However, as we've seen, Person-God metaphors are only a stopping place on the spiritual journey. Those who have gone before us tell us about the maturing process. As we grow, reducing God to a human mold restricts our souls. God cannot be limited to thinking human thoughts, doing human things, or enacting human will.

Anselm-Niagara tends to ignore the doctrine of ineffability. Its narrative limits divine love and grace to human forms. Human love and grace come in limited quantities. Even though we talk about God's unlimited love, this version of our story undercuts our words.

Unlimited divine love changes everything. If we take it seriously, we have to tell a different story. A rethought story will need a God bigger than us, a God who doesn't eventually get fed up with human sinfulness.

God is not a man, our scriptures tell us.

God's love is not human love.

God's grace is not human grace.

A story in which God doesn't think like us is hard to imagine. A story in which God doesn't have instincts like we do, and isn't moved by the impulses that move us, is more demanding. It moves us into thought-territory without roadmaps.

Any story we tell about God, sin, and salvation will be limited, but we have to do better than Anselm-Niagara. We have to do a better job of imagining the implications of unlimited love. We have to reimagine the wages of sin in light of a God who is not obligated to exact death for sin.

Problem 3: Salvation for the Individual

Originating in Western Europe, Anselm-Niagara picked up a fair amount of Western individualism. It tends to see the spiritual journey as an individual one and focuses on each person rather than the whole human race.

Focusing on the individual makes less sense as we move into the quantum era. We are coming to understand how connected everything is to everything else. As we do, individualistic spirituality feels inadequate. Quantum instincts look to the whole, not just the part.

In Anselm-Niagara each person finds him or herself in trouble with God. Each owes a debt to God for sin. Consequently, Jesus's death and resurrection solve each individual's sin problem. The cross compensates God for each individual's sin infraction.

This makes individual relief the keystone. Those who grew up with this framework usually don't even feel how limited and confining it is. Steeped in Western individualism, it never occurs to us that a bigger spiritual narrative would focus on redeeming *all* of human society, not just the individual. A bigger narrative would focus on restoring *all* of the earth to divine purpose and destiny. There's nothing about that in Anselm-Niagara.

Karl Marx called religion an opiate for the masses. It keeps us domesticated, he said, tolerant of injustice while we wait for a better life in the sweet by-and-by. When we reduce our story to individual relief from the wrath of God, Marx is pretty spot on. A story that only focuses on salvation for the individual tends to eclipse focus on the whole world. Once I pray the prayer and get my ticket punched, I just have to hang on until heaven. If I feel benevolent I'll try to get others to pray the prayer, too. But I probably won't. I'll leave that to the experts.

A narrative of individual salvation implies that a healed society, healed government, healed corporations, and healed global problems are not the point. We probably can't expect such lofty goals in this sin-infected, fallen world anyway. Justice will come when the world burns up and we stand before God. *Then* judgment will be wrought and evil destroyed.

What a distortion of Jesus's life and message!

Again, we find what we look for. If our story tells us that only the individual matters, it doesn't occur to us to work on redeeming the earth.

I meet with a lot of college kids. Steeped in quantum sensibilities, they have nothing but disdain for Christianity when they analyze the Anselm-Niagara story. It is clear to them that if they became Christians it would make them *worse* people. To them, the faith we hold so dearly makes people *less* concerned for the poor, *less* concerned for the environment, *less* concerned for the oppressed, and *less* concerned about justice.

Sadly, their critique is not without merit.

It is true that many heroic and selfless Christians are working hard every day for justice, for the poor, and for the earth. However, there is also a strain within our faith that *has* become more focused on getting people saved, and less on doing good works. There is a strain within our faith that *has* stepped back from feeding the hungry, clothing the naked, visiting the prisoner, and stewarding the earth. If our story tells us earth and society are lost causes, it makes sense that we would turn our attention to the next world.

Again, this is not the Jesus way.

Problem 4: Is That All There Is?

I want to be part of something bigger than myself. You probably do, too. Consequently, I need a story that expands my horizons, elevates my vision, and points me to a life that matters. Anselm-Niagara leaves me wanting. It's not big enough.

A God-story centered on the narrow objective of getting a few select folks to heaven after they die—that's just not a grand enough narrative to demand my life, my all.

One of the problems with Anselm-Niagara is how it reduces our grand Christian narrative:

> God was pleased to have all his fullness dwell in him [Jesus], and through him to reconcile to himself *all* things, whether things on earth or things in heaven, by making peace through his blood, shed on the cross.[1]

Other Christian salvation stories are much bigger than getting a few select individuals to heaven. Jesus, our scriptures say, carried within himself the fullness of divine life. In and through him, the purpose of God is being fulfilled, to reconcile *all* things that have been estranged from divine purpose. For Paul, through the Spirit of God and the life of Jesus, all the things on earth are being reconciled to God.

I am moved by the notion of reconciling the whole earth to God. I am stirred by the vision of reconciling everything on earth and in heaven to God. The notion that death is dispelled for everything and everybody—this moves me. In other versions of our salvation story, the work of Jesus is more global, more universal than just you, me, and a band of others who go to the right churches getting to heaven.

Problem 5: A Simplistic View of Sin

Finally, Anselm-Niagara reinforces the trivialized version of sin we spoke of earlier.

Many Christians have been taught a distinction between "sin," with a lower case "s," and "Sin," with an upper case "S." The former refers to bad things we do: lying, cheating, stealing, and so forth. The latter is the virus that infects the human soul, from which bad actions rise. Growing up in church, I was taught that sin was like chicken pox. The word or deed was the pock on the skin, but the real culprit was the original sin virus infecting the body. Yes, we do bad things, say unkind words, and commit bad actions. But these are merely symptoms of the real problem. The real problem is the sin virus that contaminates the very essence of humanity.

1. Col 1:19–20.

In those chapters we spoke of a more comprehensive view of sin. We spoke of bad actions being less an outflow of a deep, viral, defining nature, and more a reaction to illusion and false belief deep in our ego consciousness.

Anselm-Niagara was hammered out while we still thought of sin in chicken-pox terms. We didn't yet think of sin in illusion, or false-belief terms.

When sin is a virus, we look for God to be our Great Physician. When we need to be healed of an incurable disease, our spiritual lives are a quest for medicine or miracle to heal us. What we *don't* look for is truth to challenge our illusory beliefs. What we *don't* look for is the truth that will set us free.[2]

Here's an example. Many of us carry a core, visceral belief that we are not worthy of love. It's a kind of existential shame in our souls. But un-love-worthiness is such an intolerable belief that we keep ourselves from looking at it. We hide it away in our subconscious and get busy avoiding it. However, our actions and motivations show us that it's still there, always spewing up toxic instincts. When beliefs like this work as core "truths" in our souls, we unconsciously build layers of belief and action in response.

If we believe we are fundamentally un-precious, we either shrivel up and blow away, or more likely, concoct a strategy to get out there and earn ourselves some preciousness. Our most common life strategies are often just that, schemes for earning love worthiness. We work hard to be nice, be caring, speak well, or perform well in our jobs. Doing so, we keep our toxic belief at bay for a while. However, our strategies don't work for long. Inevitably, somebody gets in the way of our preciousness-earning. We lose a job and can't earn. We lose a lover and aren't admired. And as soon as our strategy stops working, the falsehood is right there to speak to us. "You're un-love-worthy!"

Under the pressure of this internal voice, we often behave badly. We take shameful shortcuts to get back on track. We say a harsh word to warn off those who are impeding our strategy. We do all kinds of pressure-driven things we regret later. In short, we commit lowercase "sins" in response to these primal falsehoods and illusions we carry.

Anselm-Niagara says nothing to this. It reduces sin to only a virus that God alone can heal. Under its influence, we look to God to change our sinful natures, but ignore the quest for truth as a way in which we are set free.

2. John 8:32.

Whatever shape we give our rethought salvation narrative, it must give full weight to our whole heritage, *all* our scriptures, and *all* the voices in our tradition. Other narratives in our tradition do give more weight to the un-limited nature of God's love. They work *with* our belief that God is love. Our reconsidered story will have to step back from the limits of an anthropomor-phic God. It will have to integrate a version of divine love that is bigger than human love. Ours will need to be a story of *unlimited* divine grace.

13

Historical Alternatives

So, we need a better salvation story.

The best place to look is in our own history, our own scriptures, our own tradition. In this chapter, we'll look at several historical, orthodox alternatives to the Anselm-Niagara story of salvation.

But remember, we're talking about things that cannot be talked about.

Before we look at any alternatives, let's remind ourselves. Any story we tell will be insufficient. No story can contain the great transcendent mystery of God.

In our daily lives it is as normal as normal can be to jump from metaphor to metaphor as the situation calls for. We call a young boy playing football a brick wall when he keeps the opposing team from advancing. As soon as he's home, we call him a horse as he hungrily scoops up all the food in sight. Later we'll call him a bear when he's grouchy and an angel when he's sweet. Each is a true statement. Each conveys important meaning. But each is untrue as well. Knowing that, we jump easily from one to another. No one metaphor is sufficient to contain the complexity of a child. Each speaks to a dimension of our experience.

Each salvation metaphor does the same. It speaks to one dimension of experience. Each grapples for words to speak to recovering from our base natures and awakening to the divine center. Each calls us to one kind of experience, but no one of them is big enough to contain the divine reality of salvation.

Despite the problems with Anselm-Niagara we saw in the last chapter, it too is a good story. We could call it the "Jesus-took-the-rap-for-me" story. It speaks to an important kind of spiritual experience. It teaches us, for example, that while God's grace is unearned, love is costly. It stirs us to gratitude for love extended to us and calls us by example to lives of self-sacrifice. It's a good story. If it weren't it wouldn't have lasted this long. As a precious part of our heritage, we don't want to throw it away. The trouble is that we have made it the *only* way we tell the story.

For most of our Christian history we have had *many* ways to tell the story of salvation. We treated them lightly. That's what you do with metaphors. We stepped effortlessly from one to another. When one broke down, we stepped back easily and used another.

Alternative #1: I Was Lost, but Now I'm Found

> If someone has a hundred sheep and one of them wanders off, doesn't he leave the ninety-nine and go after the one? And if he finds it, doesn't he make far more over it than over the ninety-nine who stay put? Your Father in heaven feels the same way.[1]

My wife, two small children, and I moved from Los Angeles to Raleigh, North Carolina some years ago. A few days after we arrived, our third son was born. It was a crazy time, compounded by the insanity of Raleigh's streets! Streets in Los Angeles were laid out by sane people. Not so in Raleigh. In L.A., streets travel in straight lines and keep their name from start to finish. In Raleigh, streets travel in arbitrary corkscrews, and change names for no particular reason. Newcomers to our city laugh with a sense of foxhole camaraderie when they tell their harrowing stories of getting lost here.

Our newborn arrived with complications. We had to take him to the hospital every other day for the first several weeks of his life. For the first few trips, my wife and I took the journey together. With two heads in the game, we got lost, but were eventually able to find our way home. The first time she took the trip alone the skies opened in a tropical rainstorm. Still reeling emotionally from moving across the country, still weak from a surgical delivery, her emotions were understandably raw. We hadn't yet learned to turn the air conditioning on in a tropical rain, so she couldn't see out of the

---

1. Matt 18:12–14 (MSG).

car. Disoriented, she got going the wrong way on one of those corkscrew roads and had no idea where she was. The rain did not let up for hours. She had no cell phone and had left her wallet at home. As she began to run low on gas she realized she didn't even know our new address or phone number.

After several hours a sign told her she was no longer in Raleigh. Panic began to overwhelm her. A glimpse of what it means to be truly lost knifed through her. Some part of her knew things would turn out well, but in those moments she experienced the piercing fear that accompanies being truly lost. It was, she told me, one of the strongest and most awful feelings she'd ever experienced.

In our GPS world, we don't often experience how awful it is to be *truly* lost. When we do, we touch a core human anxiety. Jesus's self-proclaimed mission was to come for those who are truly lost.[2] As early Christians were making meaning of their experience of him, they evoked the primal experience of being lost and then finding their way. Through the years, when we try to make meaning of our experience of the spirit of the risen Jesus, we come back again and again to the metaphor.

The lost-found metaphor is more about *experience* than theology. It is less about figuring out what God did, or how it was done, and more about describing the deep experience we have when we encounter the Divine in Jesus. We are lost, serving vice, unable to access virtue. We are lost, afraid of God, afraid our very selves are toxic. We are lost, disconnected from the indwelling breath of God that animates us. It is an awful sense of dislocation.

Knowing things are not right, some part of us yearns to find our way home, to find a place of peace, connectedness, goodness, and virtue. But try as we might, we can't find our way. Bound up in this lower version of self, we feel deeply our separation from God, truth, and Divine Life. We wander. We're disoriented. We can't find our way.

For centuries, those who have experienced Christian salvation describe it as a return to hearth and home after wandering in the wilderness. It is an experience akin to coming in from the cold, dropping our anxiety at the door, and savoring the deep relief of being where we belong. It is the experience of relief. It is the experience of joy. For many, it is such a palpable encounter, they are moved to tears.

2. Matt 15:24, Luke 19:10.

We are found. We are restored. We reconnect with the indwelling Spirit of God. We realize how safe we are. We realize what Jesus's parable of the lost sheep was about. God does not rest until we are brought home. God finds us. We are found.

It is visceral not cognitive. We *experience* God finding us. Our lives were suffocating with emptiness and meaninglessness, but the Divine comes for us. Our absence is noticed; we are missed, and God's Spirit comes for us.

We are saved.

I once read a preacher's story about playing hide-and-seek as a young farm boy. He had a place under the porch where his sister couldn't find him. She hunted in the house, the weeds, the trees, the corncrib, and the barn. He snickered to himself, "she'll never find me down here." But after a time it occurred to him, "*she'll never find me down here.*" After a while, he stuck his toe out from under the porch so her next time by she would find him.

"What did I want?" the preacher asked. "What did I really want? The very same thing you want. Isn't that true?"[3]

The deepest longing of the human soul is to be found, to find our way home. The deepest longing of our souls is to be loved, treasured, and come for. For centuries, our tradition has talked about salvation in just these terms. This is one of our cherished metaphors for sin and salvation. Our lower nature compels us to wander, lost and alone, but our God comes for us. Our God calls us home.

Those weaned on Anselm-Niagara will notice what is missing in the lost-found story. There's nothing here about a universe broken by sin. God's honor isn't offended. God's holiness doesn't demand separation from us. In fact, in this story separation from God isn't an issue. God comes *for* us "while we are still sinners."[4] There's nothing here about blood being demanded for sin, nothing about a payment needed. Divine forgiveness is just assumed. Jesus grants it *pro forma* as he did for both the criminal on the cross and the

---

3. Craddock, *Stories*, 34–35.

4. Rom 5:8.

paralytic at his feet.[5] God's forgiveness just is, freely available to anybody who wants it.[6]

In this story, salvation doesn't change our standing with God. Rather, it changes how we experience life. It brings us back to our heart's home, restores us to the self we lost along the way. It brings us back to divine love, divine purpose, the way, the truth, and the life.

Sin is neither cause for death nor separation from God. God simply comes for us, gathers us up, and carries us home. No penalty need be exacted. No blood need be shed, no fixing of a broken universe. In this version people do very little. God simply comes for us. We are children who have wandered from home and suffer the fear, anxiety, and dislocation of having done so. For no other reason than insatiable love, God comes to find us.

Alternative #2: I Was Dead, but Now I'm Alive

Like the lost-found story, the dead-alive story isn't a *quid-pro-quo* story. It is not an "if-then" affair. Neither of them insists that we do this or that so God will save us. Rather, they both tell us that help comes from God's side, not our own. In the first, he comes to find us when we're lost. In the second, he fights the death enemy we can't beat.

The story goes this way.

Our lower nature is killing us. Sin is killing us. It's a broad death that comes in many forms. Sin's blindness kills our senses so we can't see God move or sense the divine Presence. It is a soul death and a psychological one. Dreams that are born of divine destiny are killed off. Hope suffocates and dies. The same is true for virtue, wisdom, peace, and a close connection to the indwelling Spirit.

Death in all its iterations, and its traveling companion, sin, assault the human soul. Sin spawns death. Death is the wage of sin, Paul says. Intimately connected as they are, if death is conquered, sin is conquered along with it.

The good news in this story is that Jesus conquers death, and sin with it. When we experience the spirit of the risen Jesus, we embrace reality as reality is. Life is eternal. Death is a paper tiger. Life is bigger than we thought.

5. Luke 23:42–43, Mark 2:5.
6. Luke 7:47, Luke 23:34, John 20:22.

Jesus unmasks death and shows us the way things really are. Easter demonstrates the truth that there is a power greater than death. "Where is your victory?" Paul asks. "Where is your sting?"[7]

But there's more! In the dead-alive narrative, Christ doesn't just defeat sin and death himself. He becomes only the *firstborn* into a new kind of life. There is a second, third, and one millionth born as well. Jesus reveals the future set before us. For us, just as it was for him, life conquers death. By implication, life conquers sin as well.

This is a compelling story to find ourselves in. Death does not win. Sin does not win. Evil does not win. Instead, God's Spirit within us and within the entire universe wins. It is a hero story. Jesus took on death and sin, unworthiness and failure, hatred and oppression. They put up a fight, but Jesus didn't back down. He stood up for us. The fight cost him his life. It stripped him naked and cost him dearly, but he didn't back down. The system tried to silence him. Hatred tried to silence him. Blindness tried to silence him, but he didn't back down. Love hung on the cross, stood up for truth, and stood up for life. Death was exposed as a hollow threat, a straw man. Love took up the fight—and won! And now, those early storytellers proclaimed, we are liberated! We look forward with hope to life eternal and souls washed clean of sin.

> Think of it! Death defeated! Sin forgiven! The slate wiped clean. The death warrant canceled and nailed to Christ's cross. He stripped all the spiritual tyrants in the universe of their sham authority at the Cross and marched them naked through the streets.[8]

Again, notice what is missing. Death is not punishment for sin. It was an enemy we didn't know we could defeat until we saw Jesus do it. God's wrath did not need to be satisfied. Rather, God and Jesus collaborated in a cosmic battle that brought about the downfall of sin, death, law, and enslavement. And they won! The system of domination and control was overcome by love. Death and sin were revealed for the bankrupt emptiness they are.

7. 1 Cor 15:55.

8. Col 2:14–15 (paraphrase).

Alternative #3: I Was Kidnapped, but Now I've Been Ransomed

> The Son of Man," Jesus said, "did not come to be served, but to serve, and to give His life as a ransom . . . for all.[9]

In the ancient world, kidnap and ransom were different affairs than they are today. For us, kidnapping is a crime motivated by financial payoff. In ancient times things weren't quite so refined. Kidnapping was less a crime, and more a business transaction. People were kidnapped because of a need to beef up the labor pool. Kidnappers might have said, "We need workers! Let's go to war," or, "We need women to bear and raise our children. We need cooks. We need somebody to clean up around here, somebody to work the fields! Off to war we go!"

In those days, the families of those kidnapped were unwillingly thrust into a business transaction. It was a simple issue of price determined by supply and demand. If there was a strong need for labor, the ransom was dear; if the need wasn't as strong, not so dear. If the ransom was high enough, a family would have to surrender their loved one to a life of slave labor. But if they could meet the price, they could buy their loved ones back. Money talks. Everything has a price.

In this cultural context early Christians found a language to speak of their experience of salvation. Sin felt like enslavement. Enslaved to their darker angels, dominated by their lesser natures, Jesus bought their freedom. Their experience of Jesus was like ransom had been paid and they were set free! Jesus's act of selfless love and sacrifice delivered them from the compulsions and fears that had dominated them. "I'm free!" "I'm free!"

This is the way C. S. Lewis told the salvation story in his children's book, *The Lion, the Witch, and the Wardrobe*.[10] Narnia was under the control of the evil witch. Darkness and bitter cold held the whole land in icy captivity, where it was always winter, but never Christmas. The grip continued until a business transaction was struck to negotiate the land's freedom. Aslan, the great lion, made his deal with the devil, giving the witch the price she wanted, his death. The deal was struck, Aslan was killed, and the land was set free. That would have settled the affair except Aslan had a secret up his sleeve. There was, it

9. Matt 20:28, 1 Tim 2:6.

10. Lewis, *Lion, Witch*.

turned out, a magic deeper than the ransom transaction. Unconsidered in the negotiations was the magic that raised Aslan after he died. Nobody had even considered that death would not be the final word.

Many early Christians found deep meaning in this redemption story. Again, notice that the cross liberated humanity from their bondage to sin and death, but not as a penalty, not as a blood payment. A loved one (God) struck a deal to buy back the freedom of the captured. They could not meet the price themselves, so it was a rescue operation, freeing them from slavery to sin and death.

For centuries, this metaphor has pointed Christians toward growth and truth. It has stirred in us deep gratitude and wonder. It has helped us look for freedom over sin that we didn't know was possible. It has called us to divine empowerment over soul bondage and awakened in us a deep and abiding hope. Sin is not the final word. No matter how strong its grip is on us, liberty and freedom are ours to experience. It is a story of joy, gratitude, and the newness of life.

Alternative #4: I Was Weak, but Now I'm Strong

The Spirit helps us in our weakness.[11]

We human beings are weak! We all share Paul's curse. The lower self keeps winning. The higher self keeps losing. The things we want to do we cannot. We are too weak to rise above our base natures. Again and again, day after day, we succumb to our false selves.

But there is a salvation story that points to a solution to this problem. It is the "I was weak, but now I'm strong" story. This way of speaking about Christian salvation finds in Jesus, and the indwelling spirit of God, a dimension of strength we didn't know we had. Generation after generation has found itself able to "do all things in Christ who strengthens us."[12] Whereas we were once unable to muster righteousness, holiness, or a divine life, we are now able to overcome impurity and wickedness.[13]

---

11. Rom 8:26.
12. Phil 4:13.
13. Rom 6:19.

This story doesn't focus on getting God to forgive us or on restoring God's honor. It skips right over those and focuses on the way we are empowered in Christ to live higher lives. Forgiveness is simply assumed. God's honor is secure. There's no focus on death, blood, or ransom.

This story speaks about an interior, divine capacity to rise above human weakness. It tells us that the Spirit of God we saw in Jesus is in us as well. It is a source of potency we didn't know was there. Bad behavior doesn't earn us God's enmity. It just screws up our lives. Salvation is our shared experience of accessing the internal, divine strength to rise above bad things.

Our problem, this story tells us, is bigger than we have strength for.

Sin traps us and puts us into a hole so deep we can't get out of it alone. Try as we might, under sin's tyranny we are crushed. The load accumulates, daily pulling us further down. It suffocates us. It strangles us. At some point, the backlog required to change becomes so demanding we don't have the reserves to do what needs to be done. It's like we're carrying a load we can't carry. We need help. We need Another to help us carry it.

It's such a deep hole it feels like we need brand new lives, total reconstruction. We just don't have the strength for such an enormous undertaking. We're too weak. We don't have the psychic, emotional, or spiritual energy. The demand is too enormous.

The change required is a full-speed astern. We need to completely abandon the road we've been on and take a completely different one. The early Christians had a word for this radical turnaround of one's life, "metanoia." We translate the word, "repentance." It means totally turning from one's former life and living a brand new one. That is a steeper demand than we've got resources for.

Our problem is deeper that we think. Metanoia demands we unlearn everything we have ever learned, un-be everything we have become.

This is a problem!

We're just too weak to affect the kind of total renovation our souls need. So we need help. We need a friend to help us.[14]

---

14. Matt 26:41; the spirit is willing, but the flesh is weak.

Those who have told the story this way spoke of the spirit of the risen Jesus being that friend. With God's Spirit in us, we find strength that is beyond ourselves. Generation after generation has testified that this Spirit avails us of the power required for repentance, required for new thoughts, new love, new virtue, and new character.

Irenaeus, a second century Christian bishop, told the salvation story this way. He talked about the indwelling spirit of Christ helping us do things we couldn't do before. "Because of His measureless love, he [Jesus] became what we are in order to enable us to become what he is."[15]

These early storytellers didn't try to pin down too specifically how it is that we experience mystical solidarity with the risen Christ. They just told us it happens. We draw upon the indwelling presence of his spirit and find ourselves able to do what was previously impossible. In his cross and resurrected spirit we find ourselves so identified with Jesus, that we draw from his capacity and do what we couldn't do on our own.

C. S. Lewis also talked about Christian salvation this way. He used the image of children learning to write their letters. Unable to form the letters themselves, a parent holds their hands, enabling them to do what they could not. Eventually the day comes when they can do it on their own.[16] Salvation awakens us to a dimension of God's spirit and strength we couldn't access. We awaken to the Spirit *in* us giving us capacity for the glorious life that has always been our intended destiny.[17] We have such solidarity with Christ that we can love in a way we could not by ourselves, think with clarity we alone didn't have, overcome vice, and exemplify virtue in ways previously unavailable to us.

The weak-strong story invites us to relax. It encourages us to quiet our minds, our wills, and our lesser selves. It calls us to find within ourselves the indwelling presence of God's Spirit, and to let it work in and through us. In this relaxed, receptive posture, we are saved. We find God's Spirit in our deepest beings, living in our very hearts.

15. Higgins, *Christianity 101*, 237.

16. Lewis, *Mere Christianity*, 60.

17. Col 1:27.

Alternative #5: I Forgot, but Now I Remember

John Scotus Eriugena was a ninth century theologian and poet from Ireland. He was one of the most influential philosophers of the Middle Ages, well versed in the Greek and Roman classics. Coming from the north though, his Christianity was less influenced by the Roman than the Celtic worldview. When he spoke of being saved by Christ, he wasn't as influenced by Augustine, original sin, or neo-Platonic instincts.

Consequently, Eriugena spoke of salvation in Jesus as recovering lost memory. For him, when we see the life of Jesus, when we experience the spirit of the living Christ, the experience calls us back to the memory of who we truly are. He taught that salvation in Christ was a call back to our true identities. When we see the love of God manifest in Christ we are awakened from what he called "the soul's forgetfulness."[18]

In Eriugena's Celtic Christian tradition, the life and death of Jesus and the spirit of Christ within us remind us of our truest natures. They jog us back to that deepest place in us, the place deeper than our illusions and false beliefs. Sin is a slumber that has overcome us. Falsehood has caused us to forget the truth. We are like the woman in Jesus's parable who has lost a precious coin.[19] The spiritual life is a quest to remember who we are. Even when we can't remember what we seek, we carry a deep inner imperative to search. We seek what we have lost, our true, divine-center selves. And once we find them, our joy knows no limit.

In this story, the sin from which we are saved is our forgetfulness. We have forgotten our most precious truth. We have been lured away by falsehood. We are living forced, driven, coerced lives because we forget the way things really are.

Salvation then, is about being set free by truth. Missing is any need to be healed of an incurable infection. We are saved when we remember. We are saved when we seek and find God's Spirit in our very selves. Missing is any payment required for sin as a legal infraction. In its place is the quest for truth and freedom. In its place is remembering who we are and walking in newness of life because we rediscover our divine centers and live from the *imago Dei.*

18. Newell. *Book of Creation,* 88.
19. Luke 15:8–10.

If sin originates in false belief, salvation isn't about payment, offended holiness, or blood sacrifice. False belief keeps us from living in the way, the truth, and the life. It is our illusions that separate us from the indwelling spirit of God.

Alternative #6: I Was Blind, but Now I See

Jesus healed a blind man and got more than a little grief for his efforts. During the controversy, the newly-sighted man was questioned. His response articulates another of the ancient ways we have told our salvation story.

"I don't know much about how this stuff happens," he said. "There's only one thing I know for sure. I was blind. Now I see."[20]

From our earliest days, people who "are saved" compare the experience to having been blind and coming to see. Jesus demonstrated God's life and love so profoundly that our eyes are opened to life we could not see. His lavish self-sacrifice grips the depths of our hearts and opens our blind eyes. When we see Jesus extend forgiveness and goodness to his tormenters, we see the heart of God. Our eyes open. We are awakened. We begin to see through the same lens Jesus did.

The Roman centurion at the foot of the cross had his eyes opened.[21] Jesus unmasked the corruption of the old way of being, showing him the very heart of God. The centurion saw love, grace, mercy, and forgiveness in a way he had previously not been able to. He saw their potency, strength, and staying power. He saw! And in the seeing, he was changed. He was saved.

Seeing truth enables us to live differently. We see the importance of living selflessly, and discover the pathway to do so. We desire to join God in benevolence and see how to do it. We want to give ourselves to our neighbors and the world, and we realize how it can happen.

Jesus's life and death laid bare the enemies of our souls. Violence, vengeance, domination, and control were exposed for the impotence and feebleness that they are. Like a puffer fish, vice, fear, selfishness, and pride expand themselves to look daunting. But in the end, they are all show, and no substance.

20. John 9:1–41.
21. Matt 27:54.

Our vision of Jesus reorients our interior compasses and reveals the shallowness of our lesser instincts.

The way Jesus lived and died flaunted conventional wisdom. He unmasked the tired old systems that dominate so much of human life. In him, we see those systems for the hollowness and emptiness they are. Selfishness, cruelty, revenge, and judgment don't have the staying power we need in our lives. Mercy is solid. Cruelty is not. Selflessness works. Selfishness does not. The virtues that appear weak and foolish actually turn out to be strong and wise. In Jesus we *see* these divine truths and they win us over. In Jesus, we see what we hadn't seen and it changes us. As Peter said, in Christ's suffering he set an example for us. Seeing him, we are able to follow it. This saves us.[22]

Theologians call this version of our salvation story the "moral influence theory of the atonement." When Christians object to it, it's usually because it doesn't seem very dramatic. It doesn't seem powerful enough to overcome our sinful human character. Simply "seeing" Jesus doesn't seem commanding enough to root out something as deep as we believe sin is.

But our objections may reflect a limited view of how powerful *seeing* truly is. We need a bit of church history to help us rethink the power of seeing.

The East-West Split

About a thousand years ago, the church went through the Great Schism. The Western church kept its headquarters in Rome, the Eastern moved to Constantinople. There were a lot of political reasons for the split, but at the core of the divide were two fundamentally different approaches to spirituality. The Western approach was a lot about the head, the Eastern about the heart. Western thought had been deeply influenced by scholasticism,[23] a strong drive to reconcile Christian theology with Greek philosophy. Consequently, theirs was a cognitive approach, trying to eliminate mental contradictions and inconsistencies in their theology. Their approach to spirituality prioritized thinking clearly, reasoning well, and formulating clear, complete, and interlocking doctrines.

22. 1 Pet 2:21.

23. Aquinas, Anselm, Abelard, etc. were scholastics (the big names in Western Christianity).

Eastern Christians, on the other hand, felt like fish out of water in philosophical discourse. For them, following Jesus wasn't about reason at all. It was about an experience of the heart, and particularly a heart-centered way of *seeing*. They believed that spiritual sight transforms the deepest part of our souls. Theirs was a quest for the experience of the risen Christ that would open the eyes of their hearts, an epiphany that would forever change them.

They had a word to talk about this approach to spirituality, "theoria." It meant to contemplate something, to look deeply and speculate about its nature. It wasn't an empirical kind of looking. It was a heart oriented kind of observing. They emphasized terms like "the eye of the soul," insisting that if one's eye was clear, one's soul would be clear.[24] For them, spiritual awakening happened when the eye of the heart was clarified, when spiritual sight was restored.

Sin and suffering, in their view, were caused by hearts blinded by false vision. We see things one way when in fact, they are a different way. They echoed Jesus's teaching that when our light becomes darkness, our souls languish.[25] Conversely, when we come to true sight, spiritual sight, it is the very power of salvation. When we see truth, truth sets us free.[26]

Seeing saves us!

Soul sickness is a function of soul blindness. We've been captured by false truths, but when the eyes of our souls are opened, we are saved. When we see things as they truly are, we are set free. New sight makes us able to transcend sin and suffering. Awakening to new vision changes our priorities and shifts our values. Awakened to new sight, we are able to access the spirit within. We live new lives.

Jesus's selfless and exemplary life opens our eyes and calls us to draw from the same indwelling presence he did. We see past the emptiness of human power, arrogance, and pride and stop building life our own way, on our own timetable, with our own cleverness.

Both Jesus and Paul taught the "I was blind, but now I see" story.[27] Earliest Christian teachers did, too. Clement of Rome, Ignatius of Antioch, and

---

24. Matt 6:22.
25. Matt 6:23.
26. John 8:32.
27. 1 Cor 11:1, Matt 16:24, 1 John 2:6, John 13:15.

Irenaeus all taught salvation this way.[28] Origen, one of the earliest Christian leaders, wrote that having our eyes opened was so powerful that it purged us of sin and wrought deep change in our hearts.[29]

Despite its honored heritage in our tradition, many Christians today have trouble embracing "I was blind, but now I see." "Seeing" just doesn't feel powerful enough to remove the stain of sin, which is why it is so important for us to rethink human nature. We need a better salvation story than Anselm-Niagara. Our history gives us a whole bevy of them. However, before we can embrace them we need to rethink sin. Sin is not the big deal we've made it these last several centuries.

Affected by the historical view of sin as many are, it is difficult to imagine that *seeing* could be powerful enough to change our DNA (original sin). However, seeing *is* powerful. It is certainly powerful enough to shed a veneer. Until we lost our church's Eastern perspective, we knew seeing *was* powerful enough to save us.

Use Them All: They're Ours!

In the early years of our religion, we didn't approach salvation as a doctrine. We collected a basket of images and narratives to help us describe our experience. We used them to describe how we were being changed. Our philosophy was that light comes to us and we are changed. Divine word becomes flesh, love illuminates the world, and we are changed. Wounded and rejected souls are healed and invited into community. Cast-offs are loved. Untouchables are touched. We are changed.

Salvation stories point us to *experience*. For as long as we have been Christian we have testified that the death of Christ changes how we live. When we feel lost, salvation narratives point us to the experience of being found. When we feel enslaved by habit or toxic relationships, these stories help us find freedom in daily life. When blinded by anger, fear, or jealousy, narratives point us to spiritual sight. Finding ourselves in them, we look for strength when we are weak, hope when we face despair. Our stories are *about* experience, and they draw us *into* experience.

28. Grensted, *Short History,* 12–18.
29. Ibid., 67.

Our stories help us find ourselves. We hear one version or another, internalize it, and over time it changes us. In simplest terms, they all tell us we are in a hole and, in our experience of Christ, we find our way out.

C. S. Lewis wrote that before he was a Christian, he believed that the first duty of a Christian was to believe a particular doctrine about what the death of Jesus meant. However, over time he came to understand that it was not necessary at all. In fact, one could experience the benefits of being "saved" with no understanding of the doctrine at all. Sensible people, he said, know that when they are hungry they need a meal. Theories about nutrition, vitamins, or proteins get hashed out a long time after the wisdom of simply eating when we're hungry.[30]

Because it is such a deep experience, a one-dimensional story won't do. Each of the ancient stories has a place in Christian experience. Each calls us to look at salvation from a different angle. Each has a basis in scripture. Each has an advocate in history. However, no one of them is a single, comprehensive system explaining exactly how salvation happens. Salvation is bigger, richer, and more multifaceted than that. Salvation stories tell us what to look for, and that there is a great deal of experience to be found.

Entering the quantum era, we are being invited to go back into our own history and rediscover these ancient stories. We are being invited to step back from doctrinal certainty and our efforts to reduce the irreducible. Hammering out a definitive, accurate, cosmic understanding of salvation was never the point. Finding Life is the point: rising above the dark within us, living from a deeper source, and awakening to the indwelling Spirit of God. This is the point!

My Salvation and Our School District

As I write this, one of these salvation metaphors is front and center in my own experience. I am finding myself in our "I was blind, but now I see" salvation story. It is nudging me to rise above an excessive focus on me, my, and mine. I'm being saved from blindness. I have been blinded by busyness, and used that busyness to excuse my neglect of others in need.

---

30. Lewis. *Mere Christianity*, 57.

The school district in my county is embroiled in a political debate over how we'll care for our poorest and lowest achieving kids. With significantly less tax revenue, we are making some really important, value-laden decisions. My older kids are out of school now, and my remaining son has a great school. This needn't be my fight. For years these kinds of things weren't. I was a busy minister, doing "the work of God." I believed my life was just too full to be concerned about kids I didn't even know.

But following Jesus, I am being saved. A glimpse of God's love in his life and death is changing me. I used to be blind to those children whose schools weren't preparing them for fruitful and productive lives. But now I see.

It's a demanding kind of seeing. I have to follow the news, read up on school board decisions, figure out how to vote, and get involved. I have sensed an internal nudge to clear something from my calendar so I can go back to tutoring in the local middle school a couple of hours each week. As Jesus opens my eyes to God's unconditional love and acceptance, I see that all children are God's children. That includes kids on the other side of town. It's not enough for my own children to be in a good school. Jesus opens my eyes to God's love for other people's kids. And once they are opened, I see that other people's kids deserve my energies just as my own do.

Today, I am being saved from blindness.

How about you?

Rethinking What Will Happen

14

A Beautiful Story Gone Bad

Ours Is a Beautiful Story

Our Christian story is a beautiful one.

Our story of the afterlife is an inspiring one.

Again, however, it is a story too big to fit into words. It speaks of hope that defies description. It holds forth an anticipation too big to fit in mental images. Life is unlimited. It is not doled out in tiny doses while our hearts beat. Life is too big to be contained in the days of our lives.

It is also a story of conquered fear. Finding ourselves in the Christian story of the afterlife, we do not fear death. We do not fear God. We do not fear those who can take from us. We do not fear those who can take our very lives. Ours is an imperishable future.

And it is a story of things ending well. It is a story of the ultimate triumph of goodness. We anticipate a future in which our deepest purpose and longing are fulfilled. We look to the day when the God-shaped vacuum in each of us[1] is filled, and the defining hunger of our souls is satisfied. Eyes have not seen, our scriptures tell us, ears have not heard, and minds cannot imagine what it means to be fulfilled in Divine Life.[2] It is a beauty we cannot imagine.

Ours is a hope so great, it changes how we live our time on earth. Our story infuses meaning into the struggles of each day. It tells us that life is not futile.

1. Goodreads, "Pascal," para 1.
2. 1 Cor 2:9.

Our wounds are not the whole story. Missed opportunities do not define us. War, and murder, and human suffering are not the final word. Love overcomes hate. Goodness overcomes evil. Peace prevails. What is lost is restored. What is damaged is redeemed. Our story ends well.

Our afterlife story is informed by the Christian experience of Jesus. Before Jesus, reality existed in clear categories: there was death and there was life. Now however, there is a brand new category, a *death-is-not-death* category. Death is change, not the end. It is a new way of being. In Jesus's life and death we find hope for our own. Our hearts anticipate the triumph of forgiveness, goodness, love, and healing.

Jesus heralds a bright future. The perishable is trumped by the imperishable.[3] On the other side of our last heartbeat awaits something profound and wonderful. What we experienced in Jesus changed everything. Even though we stumble for words to contain the vastness of our story, we try. Death is swallowed up in life,[4] despair swallowed in hope, and sin in forgiveness. The constrained experience of life and death are shattered. The limits of time, space, and matter cannot contain existence. There is more. There is a way of being that will not fit into the limits of length, width, and height. Life is deeper, wider, bigger, more, and better than we imagined.

Through the centuries, finding ourselves in this story has often inspired us to lives of uninhibited abandon. It has inflamed our souls. We have loved lavishly and forgiven freely. When death is not the final word, we free ourselves to serve the earth without restraint. We have laid down our lives for others. We have served justice. We have served goodness. We have faced the end of our days, eyes fixed on a bright destiny. Our glimpse of Jesus inspires hope in a dazzling life set before us.

It is a beautiful story.

It is an inspiring story.

It is vague and ill-defined, but it is wonderful!

But as we've seen, history has a hard time sustaining vague or ill-defined. We just can't resist the temptation to contain the uncontainable. Even beautiful stories degrade over time. Uncontainable life gets reduced to banal images

3. 1 Cor 15:53.
4. 2 Cor 5:4.

186

that fit in our minds. We reduce our afterlife to harps on clouds and celestial choir practice. We just can't help ourselves. We take beautiful, inspiring hope, and we reduce it to gold streets, plenty to eat, and the absence of tears.

It's just what we do. When we tell and retell our stories we always try to make them a little better, a little more concrete. In our efforts to make them fit into whatever current belief we're working with, we unwittingly reduce them. We add a clock or a mansion with many rooms, and we squeeze out the mystery. We adapt the story to fit with our current thinking about sin or the nature of God, and in the adapting, unintentionally make it toxic.

We can be forgiven our temptation. Honestly, the Christian afterlife feels too good to be true. It is a story of divine love so expansive it violates human reason. It is so rich in unearned love and grace, we can't see how it could be true. Judgment, we understand—condemnation, too—but love that trumps punishment, that is beyond our experience.

So through the years of telling and retelling, we've made our afterlife story just a little more reasonable.

A Little More Reasonable

> When the Son of Man comes in his glory, and all the angels with him, he will sit on his glorious throne. All the nations will be gathered before him, and he will separate the people one from another as a shepherd separates the sheep from the goats. He will put the sheep on his right and the goats on his left.
> Then the King will say to those on his right, "Come, you who are blessed by my Father; take your inheritance, the kingdom prepared for you since the creation of the world . . ."
> Then he will say to those on his left, "Depart from me, you who are cursed, into the eternal fire prepared for the devil and his angels."[5]

In the second and third centuries, when Christianity moved west and we began interpreting our scriptures through Greco-Roman, neo-Platonic eyes, our afterlife story went through a profound shift. The way we've come to tell it through the years goes something like this.

---

5. Matt 25:31–41 (excerpts).

We die. When it happens, we line up before God's throne to face our final judgment. As we approach God, he looks into a great book where he keeps the record of our lives. Here Christians differ on how the story goes. The book might record whether we did or did not pray the salvation prayer. For another denomination it records whether or not we were baptized. For other groups the book logs whether we were "sanctified," received a "second baptism," fed the hungry, clothed the naked, or visited prisoners. In any case, it records *something*, something we did or failed to do while on earth. The book determines our status before God and whether we'll be sent to the eternal glories of heaven or the eternal torment of hell.

There is a second possibility. We might be alive during the last generation on earth. In this case, we'll hear a trumpet blast and along with all the nations of the earth, will be called to the great, final judgment. Church folk differ here, too. One group believes Christians will be whisked away to God's presence while those who remain will undergo terrible suffering. Others believe Christians will go through the terrible time along with everybody else. Still others split the difference. But in any case, there is a final judgment upon the earth and when it's done, everybody is judged; everybody's eternal destiny is determined.

Like many Christians, I grew up believing this was our story. For goodness sake, how else can we interpret Jesus's parable of the sheep and the goats?

But is it our story? Is it the one and true Christian version of the afterlife? Or is it a version of the story degraded through the years of telling and retelling.

To help us explore that question, let's first look at its problems. Whether or not it is *the* Christian story, it is certainly a problematic story.

Problem #1: Dividing "Us" from "Them"

Standing before God's final judgment at the end of our lives is a powerful, evocative image. So powerful in fact, that it has become for many the organizing principle of our religion. The focus of our spiritual energies is often a response to this image. It so dominates our minds that our spiritual lives are spent preparing for that great and powerful day. We work hard to make sure the day goes well for us, for our families, and for our friends. It creates a commanding imperative by which we live: Get to heaven! Stay out of hell!

Our spiritual efforts focus on figuring out the right prayer to pray, and the right ritual to perform, so we'll be okay in the end.

So there we are, the story tells us. We've taken our last breath and now we're standing in line, waiting for our reward, waiting to be ushered into life everlasting.

But sadly, across the way, there is another line. *We* prayed the right prayer. Unfortunately, *they* did not. *We* belonged to the right church. Sadly, *they* did not. *We* were baptized (or somehow sanctified). *They* were not. Consequently, *we* await our eternal fate. *They* await theirs.

Again, this potent image informs the life we are living here and now. Every personal interaction we have is either with somebody who will be *with us*, or with somebody who will *not*. Confident in our belief about how things end, we know the status of each one of our co-workers, friends, neighbors, and family members. They are either one of us—or they are not.

When this is our story, it plays in the background of our days. We know who the sheep are, and who the goats are. Things are clearly laid out so we know where everybody stands. We feel solidarity and camaraderie with those who are with us. Everybody else is in a separate category. They are "them." We are "us."

Growing up in church, I was warned about "them." I was warned not to have non-Christian friends or date non-Christian girls. People who loved and cared for me wanted to protect me from harm. They tried their best to keep me safe. "Them" was a dangerous category. "Them" might lure me into the wrong line. "Them" might undo all the good work "us" had done to make sure the Day of Judgment would go well.

And so, we Christians have tended to create ghetto enclaves for ourselves. We've tended to lock ourselves into echo chambers of Christian culture to keep us all together and all safe. We send our kids to Christian camps and make sure they listen to Christian music. We date on Christian websites and listen to Christian radio stations. We keep ourselves over here because "*them*" tend to hang out over there. We gather with our own kind and keep ourselves separate from the other kind.

That's what happens when we tell a two-line afterlife story.

"Us vs. them" is a pretty good indicator that our story needs rethinking. It runs completely contrary to our Judeo-Christian heritage. As far back as our captivity in Egypt we knew what it felt like to be "them." We were aliens in a foreign land, and taught one another to identify *with* the outsider, *with* "them."[6] We codified into law a deep respect for, and identification with, outsiders.[7] Solidarity with "them" has always been our way. Our ancient Hebrew tradition taught us to care for "them" deeply[8] even before Jesus taught us to love outsiders with the same passion with which we loved ourselves.[9] Jesus taught us that the heretic and outsider, the Samaritan, could be closer to God than "us."[10]

The Christian story has no place for "us vs. them." If our two-line afterlife story does, that part of our story needs some rethinking.

Problem #2: Making God a Bad Guy

We saw how the Anselm-Niagara salvation story implies a mean, capricious God. The two-line afterlife story only reinforces the idea. As we saw, an omnipotent, omniscient God is troubling. It means that God creates some people knowing they will end up in the "them" line. God creates some people for the express purpose of suffering eternal torment, perhaps as a morality tale for the rest of us. Is that just? Good? Loving? Sounds like a kid who tortures cats and pulls the wings off of butterflies.

We say God is loving and good,[11] but then we tell the two-line story. Sure, God is good today, but just wait until tomorrow! The day is coming when his judgment will be swift and harsh. People from other religions, skeptics, wonderers, and wanderers will all be shipped off to eternal torture. In the end, God's terrible judgment will carry the day. God will right the scales of justice and get even with people who didn't do right here on earth.

When we tell our story this way, in effect we're saying: "God loves you and has a wonderful plan for your life—unless you don't pray the right prayer. Then, pow! He is really going to get you! You'll be sorry."

6. Exod 23:9.
7. Lev 24:22.
8. Lev 19:33–34.
9. Luke 6:27.
10. Luke 10:25–37.
11. Ps 136:1, Rom 5:8.

God walks quietly now, but he carries a big stick for later. That impacts us! At best, we thank our lucky stars we are heading for the right line. At worst, the idea of a loving God becomes meaningless. God's acceptance is always conditional. He puts on a good face but is quietly seething under the surface, just waiting for the day when punishment will restore justice.

When our story erodes God's goodness and love, it's time for some rethinking. When our story evokes fear and abiding insecurity, it's time for some rethinking. If our two-line story undercuts the childlike abandon and security that scripture teaches is ours in God,[12] it is time for some rethinking. A good God is the centerpiece of our Christian story. Again and again our psalms sing of divine goodness.[13] Jesus proclaims it.[14] Paul does the same.[15]

The Christian story has no place for a bad God. If our two-line afterlife story does, that part of our story needs some rethinking.

Problem #3: Reducing Religion to Behavior Control

When we reduce the end of our story to final reward or punishment, we reduce God to a rewarder of good behavior and a punisher of bad. Our religion becomes exactly what our critics say it is, a thinly veiled effort to control people. Heaven and hell reward those who live well and punish those who do not. The cosmic scales of justice are balanced in the end. People who got away with murder in this life get what they deserve in the end. Our story speaks of God's grace, but grace eventually runs out. Then the truth comes out. It always *was* about justice.

In this life, good people suffer and bad people get off scot-free. That is galling. The two-line story mitigates that gall by making sure everything gets set square in the end. Virtue is rewarded and hidden sins are ultimately punished.

We're dishonest with ourselves if we don't admit a big part of our two-line story is to motivate us to behave. It's been this way as long as people can remember. From the time we Christians made our deal with the devil and

---

12. 1 John 4:7–12.

13. Pss 34:8, 73:1, 100:5, 136:1 et al..

14. Mark 10:18.

15. Rom 8:28.

became the official religion of the Roman Empire, social control has been one of the social functions of our religion. We have been on the front lines, keeping society intact, and making sure everybody lives right. And to do it, we've used the carrot of heaven and the stick of hell. It's a time-tested strategy, and it works.

Christians aren't alone in using the afterlife to fill this social function. In one of Plato's dialogues, Socrates said the same thing just before he died:

> If death were a release from everything, it would be a boon for the wicked . . . [By] dying they would be released not only from the body but also from their own wickedness.[16]

If there is no punishment after death, Plato says, wicked people will try to get away with murder. Righteous people will suffer the injustice of having their virtue unreciprocated and unrewarded. And that's just not right! For years, religious folks have told afterlife stories that do something about that! Plato did!

> The ancient and holy doctrines . . . warn us that our souls are immortal, that they are judged, and that they suffer the severest punishments after our separation from the body. Hence we hold it better to be victims of great wrongs and crimes than to be doers of them.[17]

If the two-line story was our only option, we would just have to live with a religion reduced to behavior control. It's not a bad thing, after all. I like living in a society where people behave. However, making that the *purpose* of our religion doesn't make for a very inspiring story. It certainly doesn't captivate or move us. It doesn't rouse us to the great heroism and selfless service that is part of our heritage. Behavior modification makes for a functional religion. It serves its purpose, but not a very inspiring one.

Jesus taught us that our loyalty is to a bigger story, a blowing-your-mind, kingdom-of-God story. Our loyalty is to the highest expression of divine purpose, not simply to serve the functions of civil order.[18] Even though we

---

16. Bernstein, *Hell,* 54.
17. Ibid., 52.
18. John 19:11.

work within the confines of governing authority, we are not to be its tools.[19] Paul affirmed the same.[20] So did Peter.[21]

The Christian story cannot be reduced to behavior modification or a tool to maintain civil order. If our two-line afterlife story can, that part of our story needs some rethinking.

Problem #4: Overcompensating

We tend to get louder when we feel insecure. We probably think that if we raise the voltage on our argument, it will balance out our anxiety and uncertainty. We tend to overplay our hand when we feel we're on shaky ground.

Growing up in the church, I was taught the two-line story with a great deal of seriousness and unsmiling gravity. Even as a young boy, it seemed to carry an inordinate amount of bluster and blow, with maybe a bit of harangue. When many Christians speak of the end of things, we sometimes come off sounding overly confident, overly self-assured, and maybe a little bit strident.

Nobody knows what happens when we die. Nobody knows what happens when time ends. To say otherwise is disingenuous.

All four of the corners of Wesley's quadrilateral we explored in chapter two are vague and contradictory on the point. Scripture and tradition, we will see in these chapters, are much fuzzier than we have been led to believe. Reason and experience can't even contain the idea of timelessness. What does it mean to be beyond time and space? None of us really understand the afterlife. When we insist we do, it stretches credulity.

Perhaps it is because it is an area of such uncertainty that we speak so overconfidently. To outside observers, especially those with quantum sensibilities, it must appear that we're reacting against our own doubts, swinging wildly toward certitude to compensate for insecurity.

Our uncertainty may well be the result of overstating our case. When we tell the two-line story, we speak with such concrete certainty that we have

---

19. Matt 22:15–22.
20. Rom 13:1.
21. Acts 5:29.

a hard time believing the story ourselves. When we squeeze humility and uncertainty out of our story, it doesn't serve us well.

Shrill overconfidence has no place in the Christian story. Ours is a story of humility and mystery. It *is* a potent story of goodness and hope. However, when we speak it out, our words are attempts to speak of that which cannot be spoken. When we make our story as specific and precise as our two-line story does, we overstep.

The Christian story has no place for overconfidence or bluster. If our two-line afterlife story does, that part of our story needs some rethinking.

Problem #5: Credulity

Perhaps we overcompensate because we have a hard time believing our own story. The Christian story of the afterlife faces two tough credibility issues. First, as we've seen in other instances, when we make our stories concrete, precise, and specific, as the two-line afterlife does, we work *against* quantum sensibilities. Second, good-news stories are out of sync with the dominant narratives of our day.

The quantum world is a world of uncertainty. Confident, precise, specific, concrete stories don't ring true in our newly emerging world. In our attempt to make our story better, more precise, less vague, and less mysterious, we unwittingly made it sound hollow and empty. When we say exactly what happens, exactly what God does, and exactly what happens to both us and them, we unwittingly tell a story we have a hard time believing ourselves. We don't live in a precise world any more. Precise stories sound less true. Certain stories have become harder to believe.

The bigger strain on credulity however, has to do with the dominant narratives of our day. Our story is a *hopeful* story. It is a *good* story. It has a happy ending. Good stories have fallen on hard times these days. So have happy endings.

Movies that end well don't usually win Oscars. To be taken seriously, a film usually has to point out the absurdity and darkness of the human experience. The same is true of happy songs or books. They make us feel good, but feeling good is almost a guilty pleasure. There is a sentiment afoot in both popular culture and the academy that darkness and despair are the only truly authentic human experiences. Joy and fulfillment are not as real as pain and suffering. Of course we would *like* to be happy. However, the dominate view of human experience has come to emphasize pointlessness and alienation. Happy endings feel like Pollyannaish delusion.

Consequently, any story that ends well, any story that explodes with boundless hope, has a hard time competing in today's marketplace of ideas.

In the nineteenth and early twentieth centuries, a group of philosophers began to frame human experience around the term "existentialism." There was some variety in how dark they were in their assessment of the human condition, but they all had the same starting point. "We exist. That's all. We exist." Reality begins and ends with human experience. Anything bigger than human existence is inaccessible, and therefore not relevant. Everything begins and ends with the thoughts I think, the feelings I feel, the decisions I make, and the life I make for myself.

That was a hundred years ago, about the same time physicists were upending our universe.

Over the last century, the seed of existentialist thought has tended to bear two kinds of fruit. The first is a form of institutionalized despair. With nothing more than "we exist" to build on, and with nothing more than faulty human nature to work with, most existentialists feel depressed and anxious. "Angst" and "despair" are the words they use. This is why all the smart films today end badly. This is why intelligent books today focus on the darkness of human existence. The residue of existential philosophy has a strong grip on our culture. Happy endings have fallen on hard times.

The second fruit of existentialism tends to be hedonism. "Life is without purpose or meaning, so let's buy some really bitchin' threads." It is not surprising that after the Second World War, our society shifted fervently to a consumer driven economy. If life *is* despair, you can never really get what you truly want. You'll have to settle for a new smartphone and granite countertops.

These are the stories Westerners are telling themselves.

They are not, however, the Christian story. Ours is a story of hope.

Existentialism, nihilism, and hedonism are stories. That's all: stories. They are stories without a happy ending, filled with angst and despair. But that is all they are—*stories*.

The Christian story is struggling to compete today. First, we overplayed our hand. We squeezed out mystery, told it in concrete, precise terms, and rendered ourselves irrelevant in the quantum era. Second, we haven't fully understood our true competition, a deep undercurrent of institutionalized despair. Our story has always seemed too good to be true. This is even more pronounced in our troubled, hopeless, and worried world of post-existentialist instinct.

Let's return to the question we began with.

The answer is no! The two-line story is *not* the one and true Christian story of the afterlife.

It can't be. These are not surface problems. They undercut the very viability of our faith. As Christians we *cannot* abide us vs. them. It is counter to everything we stand for. We *cannot* abide a bad-guy God. It too, goes contrary to the very center of our faith. We *cannot* reduce the irreducible, we *cannot* turn good news into bad, and we *cannot* acquiesce to the dominant narrative of the day.

We clearly got something wrong along the way. This *cannot* be our story.

Our two-line story may help us die well, but it does not help us live well. When we reduce our whole narrative to a really big judgment to settle all accounts, we reduce our spiritual lives to getting ourselves ready to die.

But we are Christians. We have a powerful story. Hanging on until we go to heaven—that is *not* powerful. Other generations of Christians lived from a better story, a story that exploded fear and inspired them to change the world.

Something went wrong. Something needs to be rethought.

15

Fuzzier than We Thought

Yes. The two-line story is fraught with problems. However, it has been around a very long time. It holds such a cherished place in our heritage; how dare we rethink it? To do so evokes in many a deep sense of guilt, disloyalty, or fear of heresy.

Christians are inheritors of a rich heritage. We have sacred texts, a deep wisdom tradition, ancient liturgies, and hard-fought theologies. We're hardly in a position to dismiss these simply because we don't like them. Our instinct is to preserve the legacy given us. Even when we see problems like those in the last chapter, it feels arrogant to challenge the wisdom of those who have gone before us.

So what gives us permission to rethink our story?

On what grounds do we question so central a part of our tradition as our two-line afterlife story?

Fuzzier than We Thought: Two Worldviews. One Story

Growing up, I believed our afterlife story was one of the bedrock certainties of our faith.

It is not.

It is not the given I was led to believe. It turns out we've interpreted the texts we used to build this story through a skewed lens. We built our narrative on a foundation of sand by removing "afterlife" texts from their historical context.

The scriptures from which we have fashioned our afterlife narrative are embedded in larger arguments that are rooted in a particular time, culture, and collective experience. To get the story we tell today, we had to remove them from the thick layers of context that made them what they are. When we did, we fundamentally changed their meaning. We divorced them from the worldview in which they were written, and read into them meanings that were never part of their original context.

As we've seen, when Christianity moved west it left behind the Jewish worldview. However, Jesus, Paul, and the authors of our scriptures were Jewish. They thought about life, God, and the spiritual journey in Jewish terms, and wrote those texts from within their worldview. As such, they venerated the created world, and celebrated that God had pronounced the world and everything in it good. In the Jewish mind all of creation is good. Society is good. The human body is good. Food, sleep, sex, and community: it is all good. In the Greco-Roman mind on the other hand, creation is bad. The material world is derivative and corrupt, a contaminated place, an unpleasant holding tank where we wait to ascend to God's true and perfect world.

The texts from which we fashion our afterlife story were written by Jewish people with a Jewish worldview. However, they were *interpreted* for us by Greco-Roman people with a neo-Platonic worldview. Taken out of context, their meaning has been fundamentally altered. Our story has become one of escape rather than redemption. When the material world is irredeemable, what else can we expect?

Filtered through Greco-Roman interpretations, our faith lost the deep instinct that God was at work redeeming and healing the precious material world. It was replaced with the instinct that God was at work helping us escape the material world. One view insisted God was healing a broken world. The other insisted God was planning to burn it up, and rescue a few of us from it.

As these two languages, cultures, and worldviews were colliding, we Christians were hammering out our story of the afterlife. Consequently, we interpreted texts written in one worldview through the lens of another. We framed a story about the end of things by forcing words from one language into the instincts of another.

When the authors of scripture spoke of the future, theirs was an expectation that it was the near future, and that it would happen here, in this place.

Theirs was an expectation that God would unfold history decisively on a foreseeable timetable, and that divine restoration would unfold on the earth.

When our Jewish authors spoke of end things, a coming day of judgment, God's wrath, *Gehenna*, or a new heaven and new earth, their words came with an embedded expectation that it would be a redemptive work, a repairing of the here and now. Theirs was not an expectation that time itself would end or that the earth would be destroyed. Theirs was the expectation that an *epoch* would end, a time of injustice, oppression, or evil would end, and the hand of God would bring about liberation.

If we want to understand what our afterlife texts meant to Jesus and their authors, it will require some detective work.

We have to unearth *their* worldview, set aside our own, and interpret these texts accordingly. We have to position ourselves in the minds of the authors and read through the lens of *their* history, *their* cultural assumptions, and *their* societal norms. If we want to understand our own scriptures, we have to keep asking what they meant when they were written, not today.

We saw earlier that the kingdom of God was a central theme of Jesus's teaching. In his worldview, it was clearly understood that the kingdom was a here-and-now experience.[1] However, subjected to Greco-Roman interpretation, it became for many a faraway place, in a faraway future, when time has come to an end.

The historical shift from one worldview to another has made our afterlife story much fuzzier than we thought. The clash of two worldviews has left us a legacy of confusion regarding the afterlife. This confusion both invites us and gives us permission to rethink our story.

Fuzzier than We Thought: The Dead Sea Scrolls

We have a whole bevy of scripture texts we cite to tell our story of the afterlife.[2] We quote wild prophesies from the books of Daniel and Revelation. We speak of mansions with many rooms,[3] a lake of fire,[4] a new heaven and

---

1. Mark 1:15, Luke 11:20, 17:21.
2. Matt 10:28, 25:46, Mark 9:43–48, Luke 23:43, 16:23, John 14:2.
3. John 14:2.
4. Rev 20:14.

earth, gates of pearl,[5] and chains of gloomy darkness.[6] These images hold a deep and visceral place in our hearts, they are clear in our minds, and our interpretations have been vetted through the centuries. For a long time, we felt set and secure with them.

And then we discovered the Dead Sea Scrolls.[7]

It is difficult to overestimate how our mind-maps have been exploded by archeological finds in the mid-twentieth century. Scholarship is demanding we undertake a fundamental overhaul of our understanding of Jesus and his teachings. This is particularly true of our afterlife story. There is simply too much new information out there for us to keep holding on to our traditional story of how things end.

The Dead Sea Scrolls broadened our understanding of the ancient genre of Jewish apocalyptic literature. In this literature, Jewish peoples, long op- pressed by foreign powers, used fantastic and veiled images—celestial trumpets, bowls of plagues, floating wheels, and apocalyptic dragons—to speak of their aspirations for freedom. They used this secreted language to avoid persecution under oppression. It was a form of indirect language and symbolic imagery that helped them articulate their yearning for freedom without incurring even more oppression and injustice.

As scholars interpret our texts through the lens of these new discoveries, we are coming to understand that the authors of scripture were thinking very little about the end of space and time as Greco-Romans imagined it. Their focus was on the end of their current season of suffering. Theirs was an aspiration for the end of the epoch in which the Romans, Babylonians, Assyrians, or others were oppressing them. When they spoke of "the day of the Lord,"[8] or "the judgment of God,"[9] they did not have the Western idea of time itself coming to an end. They did not imagine the material world pass- ing away. Rather, they instinctively assumed that God's good earth would be repaired, and that God's redemptive work would bring the current age of op- pression to an end. When they spoke of a new heaven and a new earth they imagined God redeeming and restoring the *old* heaven and the *old* earth.

---

5. Rev 21:1–25.

6. 2 Pet 2:4.

7. The same is true of the discovery of the gnostic library at Nag Hammadi in 1945.

8. Isa 2:12, Amos 5:18–20, 2 Cor 1:14, 1 Thes 5:2.

9. Matt 3:7–12, 13:40.

Peace would prevail in the new era, justice would be served, and what God had pronounced "good," would be made good once again.

These discoveries and this new interpretive lens put us in a bit of a bind. We have a long and storied tradition that tells the afterlife story one way. Now, we also have these discoveries pressing us to think another way.

Our afterlife story is fuzzier than we thought. This gives us permission for the rethinking task before us.

Rethinking the Sheep and the Goats

The sheep-goat-throne story we began with is a dramatic scene. Reading the text evokes powerful images of the Son of Man coming in glory, angels in tow. He sits on a powerful throne with all the nations in attendance. Judgment proceeds with pomp and grandeur. The picture is powerfully evocative to Western sensibilities. It just *feels* otherworldly. It *feels* transcendent. It has a very *end-of-time* vibe.

But if we interpret the text in the Hebrew worldview[10] it becomes a very different story. Judgment, the text says, was being passed on "the nations," on geo-political units. The time was coming, Jewish ears would have heard in Jesus's parable, when God would set right the injustice and oppression they were suffering at the hand of Rome. The text echoes a theme from the book of Joel.[11] The day would come, Joel prophesied, when the nations would be put on trial for their mistreatment of Israel. They would be required to stand and look on as the fortunes of Israel were restored. The aspirations Joel articulated six hundred years earlier, Jesus articulated in the story of the sheep and the goats. Here again, Israel was standing on the hope that divine judgment would be passed on those who oppressed them, that God would restore their freedom and their divine inheritance.

---

10. Notice the similarity between this account in Matthew and the apocalyptic vision in Daniel 7. The Daniel passage evokes the same sense of transcendent finality, but is a reference to judgment being passed on a nation that has made war against Israel. The similarity challenges our Western feel of the end of time. Jesus joins Hebrew tradition, and calls upon God's judgment of those nations who don't help Israel advance its divine cause here on earth.

11. Joel 3:1–3.

Notice what the story was *not* saying to Jewish ears. It was not saying that all the people of the earth would line up before God at the end of time to hear how they would be spending their afterlives.

Rethinking the Parable of the Weeds

> The one who sowed the good seed is the Son of Man. The field is the world, and the good seed stands for the people of the kingdom. The weeds are the people of the evil one, and the enemy who sows them is the devil. The harvest is the end of the age, and the harvesters are angels.
>
> As the weeds are pulled up and burned in the fire, so it will be at the end of the age. The Son of Man will send out his angels, and they will weed out of his kingdom everything that causes sin and all who do evil. They will throw them into the blazing furnace, where there will be weeping and gnashing of teeth. Then the righteous will shine like the sun in the kingdom of their Father. Whoever has ears, let them hear. [12]

Western ears assume they know exactly what Jesus meant by this story. The end of time, the end of the universe is coming. When it does, the good seeds (Christians) will be harvested and will go to heaven to shine like the sun. The evil seeds (non-Christians) will be cut down and thrown into the fires of hell. It's another way of telling the two-line story.

While that *is* how Western ears would have heard the parable three hundred years after Jesus told it, it is *not* how Jewish ears would have heard it when he did. Understanding apocalyptic parables and their rooting in a this-worldly context, his audience would have heard something like this:

> Jewish authorities (Pharisees, Priests, and Herodians) are resisting the message I'm bringing. Unwittingly, they are resisting the very purposes of God. The day is coming when they will be judged for their ignorance and resistance. This current moment in history, this "age" of suffering, sin, and injustice under Rome, will soon come to an end. When it does, God will restore our people. God will restore justice and goodness. On that day those who have resisted God's purposes, those who have done evil, will be weeded out. Their failure will be exposed and their evil deeds punished.

12. Matt 13:36–43.

> Then they'll be sorry! Then they'll wish they had gotten on
> board with us. There will be weeping and gnashing of teeth as they
> realize the error of their ways. They will have missed out on his-
> tory's greatest turnaround story. They will have missed out on the
> restored, redeemed, God-kingdom that is coming to our land.

Again, this interpretation describes a time and place here on earth. It is a
this-worldly parable, predicting God's work in the not too distant future.
Jesus's Jewish audience would not have heard his parable as a judgment for
all people at the end of time. There would have been no sense that it was a
metaphor for timeless suffering at the close of history.

Rethinking a Jesus-Saying: "Fear the One Who Can Throw You into Hell"

> I tell you, my friends, do not be afraid of those who kill the body
> and after that can do no more. But I will show you whom you
> should fear: Fear him who, after your body has been killed, has au-
> thority to throw you into hell (Gehenna). Yes, I tell you, fear him.[13]

Once again, Western ears can't help but hear in this text eternal judgment
in the afterlife. But without our "everything burns," instincts, Hebrew ears
would have heard it very differently.

Many translations use the word "hell" in the text. Others leave the word in its
original language. *Gehenna* is a real place in Israel. It is *not* hell as we think of
it today. It is *not* a lake of fire in the afterlife where people go for all eternity.
It is a valley to the southwest of Jerusalem. It is a valley with a history.

In the book of Jeremiah, the prophet makes a dire prediction about the
people of Israel. Because they have worshipped detestable idols and de-
filed God's name, they will face severe judgment as a foreign nation makes
war upon them. In that war, their bodies will be thrown into the Valley of
Hinnom. So many will end up there, it will become known as the Valley of
Slaughter (*Gehenna*). Suffering God's judgment at the hands of an enemy
nation, their carcasses will become food for the birds and wild animals, and
any sounds of joy and gladness once heard in Jerusalem will be no more.[14]

---

13. Luke 12:4–5.

14. Jer 7:30–34.

It's a harsh judgment to be sure. But it is *not* a reference to timeless, disembodied suffering in eternity. Jesus is speaking of something that will happen at a specific time and in a particular place. The Valley of Hinnom (*Gehenna*) became known in Jewish tradition as the place bodies get thrown and burned in disgrace and ruin.

When Jesus referred to *Gehenna*, he and his audience all understood the context of Jeremiah's prediction. They all understood that Jesus was invoking the judgment of God to oppose those who would resist his kingdom message.

Just before he said these words, Jesus was preparing his disciples to carry his message to outlying regions of Israel. There was real threat involved in their mission. The temple authorities might well have killed them. But Jesus was telling them not to be afraid. Even if they were killed, they had nothing to fear. They were about the business of God's kingdom and would be vindicated as martyrs when the Son of Man took his kingdom.[15]

However, the judgment faced by those who rejected their message would be far worse than a martyr's death. They would not only face death for their bodies, but also the punishment of God reserved for those who resist him. Like the Israelites who resisted God in Jeremiah's time, their bodies would be killed, but worse. They'd be thrown into the Valley of Hinnom, into *Gehenna*.

The disciples would know a noble death. The deaths of their adversaries would be ignoble. There is a death that is vindicated by God, the death of the martyr. On the other hand, there is the shameful death of those who resist God's purposes. These would have their bodies thrown into the valley of dishonor to be burned, a consequence of their disregard for their God.

This is bad! But it is not the eternal, conscious suffering in hell that Westerners imagine when they read Jesus's words.

Almost all of the texts upon which Christians have built our traditional story of the afterlife lend themselves to this same kind of reinterpretation. Once we step out of the Greco-Roman perspective into the Hebrew one, they tell a very different story. When we put them back in their original context, they tell a story of here and now, not timeless judgment. Andrew Perriman has

15. Luke 12:8–12.

done a blog and book that goes systematically through each text we have used to construct our traditional two-line version of the afterlife. In each case, he shows how the Jewish narrative radically changes our story.[16]

In broad terms, our scriptures do not say what we thought they said about the afterlife. At best, the two-line narrative doesn't take into account the historical factors that inform their meaning. At worst it has been misleading us for centuries. If we would be faithful to our texts, we must hear them *within* our physical world, *within* history, not after it is all over.

We began this chapter asking this question: What gives us permission to rethink our story?

This does! The combination of the fuzziness of our story, and our unawareness of the historical factors that have informed how we have told it—*this* gives us permission for the rethinking task before us.

---

16. See: Perriman, *Heaven and Hell,* and his blog, www.postost.net.

16

Shall We Keep the Afterlife in Our Story?

Again with the Ineffable?!

If our traditional afterlife story was formed as one worldview was being forced on another . . .

If our cherished beliefs about the end are actually distortions forged by that tortured process . . .

Should we even *keep* the afterlife in our story?

As biblical scholarship unravels everything we thought we knew about end things, should we just jettison the idea altogether?

When the certainty we once had about the afterlife is shrouded in ambiguity, should we simply dispatch it to the domain of the unknowable and irrelevant?

Jesus didn't.

Questioned on the subject,[1] he indicated his belief in *something*. What he didn't do was give much texture to what that *something* might be like. Religious leaders of his day were locked in a great debate. One group said there was nothing on the other side of the grave; the other disagreed. To make their point, the first group posited a man married to seven women in his life. Imagining how ludicrous this poor man's afterlife would be was all the case they felt they needed to make.

1. Mark 12:18–27.

Jesus agreed with the absurdity of the notion, but did not dismiss the idea of an afterlife. He insisted that there is *something* on the other side of the grave, but surely not *that*. Marrying, giving in marriage, living life the way we live it on earth, whatever the afterlife is, it is not *that*.

If we are to keep the idea of an afterlife as part of our Christian story, we will be well served returning to Jesus's two basic principles. First, there is something, not nothing. Second, we don't know much about that something.

Here again, is mystery. Here again, if we are to retell our story for the quantum era, we must respect the ineffable. Incomprehensibility and the paradoxical are back. They've always been here. What has changed is our recognition of how important it is to honor them. Our newly-shaped universe is placing this wisdom of our ancestors front and center. Jesus understood the importance of mystery. Nowhere is this more important than in framing our story of the end.

Consider the story of a turtle and a fish. The two lived together in a lake. Curious about life outside the lake, the fish asked the turtle to go out for a walk and report back what he experienced. For many days the turtle explored the world outside the lake. He walked on dry sand, walked through fields of grass, and felt the wind blow in his face. When he returned, the fish asked for a report.

"Well," the turtle replied, "dry sand is nothing like water. Grass and trees are nothing like a lake. Walking in the air is nothing like swimming in water."

"Don't tell me what dry land is *not* like!" the fish insisted. "Tell me what it *is* like!"

"Well," the turtle replied, "I'm at a loss for words."

"Well, is dry land wet?" the fish asked.

"No it is not."

"Is it cool and refreshing?"

"No it is not."

"Are there ripples and waves?"

"No there are not."

"Well then," the fish concluded, "dry land must not be real."

"That is possible," said the turtle as he left for another walk.

If we are going to keep the afterlife as part of our Christian story, it will have to be in terms of mystery. We'll have to set aside our tendency to tell stories with clocks and mansions and streets. We'll have to leave big swaths of our story fuzzy and incomprehensible.

We will do well to be the turtle. "It's not like that . . . or that . . . or that." We are human. We will do well to remember our temptation to be the fish. "Don't tell me what it *isn't* like; tell me what it *is* like!" We always want a better story!

Imagination breaks down when we consider reality beyond time and space, beyond the world we live in each day. In a dimension where moments no longer exist before or after this one, what does meaning mean? Can we really speculate about life that inhabits a dimension beyond the limits of imagination?

Any story about the afterlife is an attempt to talk about that which cannot be talked about. All our speculations are just that, speculative. Once again we must resist the temptation to reduce the irreducible to an idea that will fit in our brains. We must heed the wisdom of earlier Christians and honor mystery and the unknowable unknown.

So—shall we even *keep* the afterlife in our story?

Yes, we should. However, it will require some rethinking. Let's consider a few factors that may inform the rethinking task.

Shall We Keep the Afterlife? Quantum Weirdness

Our Enlightenment temptation has been to reduce reality to what we can experience with our five senses and explain with logic and reason. In our new quantum universe, reality doesn't work that way. Mystery, the unknowable unknown, and the inexperienceable are making a comeback. A solid reality is giving way to transforming states, excited vibrations, ever-morphing energy fields, probabilities, and chaos.

We used to think that if something could not be seen, touched, felt, or reasoned, it was less real. Now we understand that less and less of what is real *can* be measured, experienced, felt, or reasoned out. "Real" no longer means solid. It means something bigger, more mysterious.

As this happens, we are becoming more tolerant of speculation about the unmeasurable nature of life beyond life. Astronomers and physicists have recently begun to speculate about dark matter and dark energy. We can't measure or see them; we just know that there's too much gravity in the universe to be explained by what is there. So we speculate about a reality beyond the reality we can measure. As we get more comfortable with this kind of thing, it becomes easier and easier to speculate about that which cannot be measured. As Enlightenment reductionism loses some of its influence, it becomes easier and easier to speculate about that which cannot be seen.

A universe increasingly rich in mystery and uncertainty argues for keeping the afterlife in our story.

Shall We Keep the Afterlife? The Mystery of Human Consciousness

Human consciousness has come into being over a very long time. It has been a wild ride! First there was a big explosion of energy. Then there were inanimate elements, then molecules, and eventually living tissue. Finally there was objective and subjective conscious awareness.

It's been a fantastic journey from inert molecules to conscious awareness. You and I are thinking thoughts together on this page. How wild is that? We are imagining one another, creating abstractions in our minds, and conjuring mental constructs that transcend the molecules and energy that make us up. We are imagining, speculating, reasoning, and conceiving. Bodies made out of physical, material stuff are able to generate experience that *transcends* physical, material stuff.

Out of stardust has emerged the experience of nonmaterial awareness. If we didn't live in it every day we'd be floored by the majesty and miracle of consciousness. How is it that we can do this thing? How can I be thinking, imagining, or existing outside myself, watching myself?

This great mystery informs the question before us. Shall we keep the afterlife?

The mystery of human consciousness is baffling. What *is* it? Where does it exist? Is consciousness made out of something? Is it made of atoms and molecules or does it exist beyond them? Is it limited to brain matter, or is brain tissue a medium that can play consciousness the way an mp3 player plays a song?

Scientists and philosophers are having a hard time answering these questions.[2] They have divided themselves into two schools of thought, the "idealists" and the "materialists." The materialists argue that everything that there is, consciousness included, can be described in terms of the properties of energy and matter. They believe these properties are expansive enough to explain all the reality there is to explain. Consciousness then, is a function of the interplay between protons, electrons, molecules, complex tissues, and electrical impulses. Human thought, individual personality, conscious awareness, and the whole of reality can all be explained in terms of physical, material properties.[3]

Idealists agree with materialists to a point. They agree that consciousness *does* exist in the physicality of the human brain. However, they argue, it *also* transcends the limits of physicality. While material substances can *contain* consciousness, they argue, the mystery of this deep human experience cannot be fully explained within their limits.[4]

Enlightenment sensibilities are fond of mechanical explanations, particularly the idea of a set of simple principles that govern the whole of reality. Consequently, when Newton was king, it was tempting to think of human consciousness in purely physical terms. Human beings, in this view, consciousness included, are like machines. We just need to figure out the equipment and how it works. This is the bias most neuroscientists bring to their work. They do brain scans to explore neural events. Figuring out what goes on in people's brains, they assume, explains the machine, and explains consciousness.

Quantum sensibilities, on the other hand, are less captivated by mechanical, reductionist certitude. In the quantum era, we *know* the universe is an uncertain place, much weirder and more complex than we thought. When we have the subjective experience of the color navy blue, or are deeply moved

2. Chalmers, "Consciousness."
3. Campbell, "Consciousness," 2.
4. See Chalmers, "Facing Up," and Nagel, "Bat."

by a piece of music, we have to ask, "What makes our inner life so rich? Can all that depth of experience be explained solely as the aggregation of neural processes?" Idealists suggest it cannot.

As we wonder if the afterlife should remain part of our Christian story, we do well to engage the current debate about human consciousness. Which of the views makes more sense? If the materialist perspective does, if the properties of protons and electrons explain all the reality there is to explain, an afterlife doesn't make sense. When the molecules in the brain unravel, consciousness must simply stop existing.

If, however, this sea of consciousness we swim in every day exists in a dimension beyond energy and matter, we ought to not shut the door to the idea.

Shall We Keep the Afterlife? Reality Beyond Reality

The materialist-idealist debate about the nature of consciousness is a subset of a bigger debate about the very nature of reality. Physicists, biologists, and philosophers are struggling with ontology, our understanding of the nature of existence.[5] Is the reality we can see, touch, and access through reason the only reality there is? In the Enlightenment worldview, a closed system with all the causes and effects tidily accounted for made sense. In our quantum world, the very idea of knowability has become suspect. We're not even sure what reality is.

First year philosophy students often encounter this thought experiment. It raises questions about the limits of human perception. If you and I look at a dollar bill, we both agree it is green. However, what we don't know is if we are having the same experience. Is your experience of green really the experience I would have called yellow? I can't be inside of you, I can't see through your eyes, so I can't ever know. And if I can't know what you are perceiving, can I be sure my own perceptions are real or true? No, I can't.

Consequently, we are faced with the uncomfortable suspicion that what you and I call "reality," is in fact, only our *perception* of reality. If there is a capital "R" version of Reality out there, I do not have access to it. I only have access to my own *perceptions*.

5. Randrup, "Idealist Philosophy," para. 29–44.

As we become more comfortable with uncertainty in the quantum era, this is not as troubling a notion as it was for our Enlightenment predecessors. That we live and work within the limits of our own perceptions is not that big a problem on this side of Heisenberg and Einstein.

And in fact, it shouldn't be difficult for us as Christians, either. Being limited to our perception is just another way of talking about our doctrine of ineffability. What we call "reality" is really just a collection of our perceptions. We *cannot* speak about Reality, only about our perceptions and experiences.

This brings up a critical question for deciding to keep or abandon the afterlife. Is there a capital "R" Reality behind our perceptions? Is there *something* that *is* Real behind the limits of our perceptions?

The question presents two options. First, there is *no* Reality behind our perceptions, in which case, the idea of an afterlife could just as well be abandoned. But second, if there *is* a Reality behind our perceptions, it is not unreasonable to imagine the afterlife connecting to it.

As the quantum era continually expands our universe and reality becomes bigger, broader, wilder, and more mysterious, the materialist perspective feels more and more constraining. When the idealists suggest the viability of a dimension of existence beyond human perception, it seems more fitting, more humble, less arrogant, and less Enlightenment era certain.

Shall We Keep the Afterlife? Near-Death Experiences

I used to think near-death experiences (NDEs) were the domain of cranks, the same kind of people who had Elvis sightings. However, as research mounts, they seem less paranormal and more statistically credible. *The Lancet* published a study that found about eighteen percent of people resuscitated from cardiac arrest had experienced a NDE.[6] They all remembered details that had happened during their heart attacks even though they had been clinically dead. Their brain stems had ceased activity, yet they continued to have awareness, often observing doctors and nurses trying to resuscitate them.

The study compiled patient experiences to determine the defining elements of a "classic NDE." These elements include a sense of peace and well-being as the center of being relocates outside the body. Many report a "tunnel"

6. Van Lommell, "Near-death."

experience, sensing themselves moving away from their bodies toward light. They often report experiencing a review of their lives, accompanied with an intense feeling of unconditional love. These, and a deepened sense of the nature of things, often cause a deep reluctance to return to their bodies.

In study after study, people who report an NDE have these same experiences. Even people who have been blind all their lives report "seeing" the same kinds of things.[7] Patients report these things even though they are having no corresponding neural activity. The brain is not working, but consciousness is.

Skeptics suggest these experiences can be attributed to biological causes: oxygen deprivation, a flood of chemicals in the blood, dreamlike states, or the power of religious suggestion. However, researchers point out that the absence of neural activity makes the idea of a dream or chemically induced hallucination problematic. In one study patients were monitored for lack of oxygen. Those who had NDEs had the same oxygen levels as those who did not.[8] Further, it seems contradictory for patients to experience heightened, lucid awareness as their brain devolves. One would expect awareness to fragment as hearts stop and brain stems cease activity.

Elements of the classic NDE are reported consistently across cultures,[9] history,[10] and religious traditions.[11] The regularity of these reports makes them increasingly difficult to dismiss. Again and again, consciousness seems to function independently of brain activity, challenging the materialist view of consciousness. When the brain stops functioning, consciousness should have drifted into nothingness, but evidence keeps suggesting something else.

An anecdote from one of the studies is particularly capturing.

7. Ring, *Mindsight*, 1–15.

8. Hope, "Near-death," para 4.

9. D'Souza, *Life*, 53-62. NDEs were reported in *Plato's Republic*, by The Venerable Bede (7th century), in the *Tibetan Book of the Dead*, by Earnest Hemingway (1918), and Carl Jung (1944).

10. Williams, "Analysis," para. 13. One notable report comes from A.J. Ayer, noted philosopher and atheist. After a heart attack, he had a NDE, saw the light, the whole thing. Afterward, he didn't back away from his atheism, but he did say that the experience "slightly weakened my conviction that my . . . death will be the end of me, though I continue to hope that it will be."

11. Shushan, *Conceptions*, 37-53.

Another remarkable case involved a Seattle woman who reported a near death experience following a heart attack. She told social worker Kimberly Clark that she had separated from her body and not only risen to the ceiling but floated outside the hospital altogether. Clark did not believe her, but a small detail the woman mentioned caught her attention. The woman said that she had been distracted by the presence of a shoe on the third-floor ledge at the north end of the emergency room building. It was a tennis shoe with a worn patch and a lace stuck under the heel. The woman asked Clark to go find the shoe. Clark found this ridiculous because she knew the woman had been brought into the emergency room at night, when she could not possibly see what was outside the building, let alone on a third-floor ledge. Somewhat reluctantly, Clark agreed to check, and it was only after trying several different rooms, looking out several windows, and finally climbing out onto the ledge that she was able to find and retrieve the shoe.[12]

History has thrown us a curve. We thought the afterlife was a bedrock part of the Christian story. But biblical scholars have taken certitude off the table. In the tumult, we're having to ask ourselves a question Christians never imagined would be up for discussion, "Shall we keep the afterlife in our story?"

Jesus kept it. And now, quantum weirdness, the mystery of human consciousness, perception, and NDE research suggest the same. These areas challenge the reductionist view held over from our Enlightenment instincts. To abandon the idea of an afterlife, we would have to ignore those areas of inquiry that suggest its viability. They were easy to overlook when our universe was a closed system governed by precise, mechanical laws. However, as quantum instincts take deeper hold, it makes less and less sense to ignore them. It makes more sense to expand the possibilities of human experience into some dimension of human consciousness that exists beyond our brains, beyond our days on this earth.

12. D'Souza, *Life,* 63.

17

Hammering Out a Better Story

For better or worse, the idea of the afterlife informs how we live our days on earth. As we've seen, even when we abandon the afterlife and reduce reality to fit in the "we-exist" story, that too informs how we live.

The scandal of the Christian story has always been that it is too good to be true. Its most fundamental premises stretch credulity to the breaking point. Death is not the final word? Oh sure. God's fundamental nature is love and grace? Oh, come on! It's all just too incredible! Our story is just a little *too* good to take seriously. It needs to be toned down a bit for us to be able to really hear it.

- Sin and death are paper tigers. Too good to be true.
- God is not punitive. Too good to be true.
- Forgiveness is simply the nature of things. Too good to be true.
- We have nothing to fear. It's all just too good to be true.

Like the early Christians, we can live our lives with abandon, fearing neither enemy nor those who can take our lives. That's what our story did for them. But when we believe it too good to be true, we tend to reduce it, shrink it, make it less scandalous, less inspiring.

Jesus carried the divine nature within him, and we do too. Too good to be true.

The Spirit of God is in you and me just as it was in Jesus. Too good to be true.

The divine nature animates and makes us "us." Too good to be true.

And the most scandalous of all is our story of the afterlife.

But if, instead of shrinking it to fit in a "just-good-enough-to-feel-true" box, we allow it to run free in all of its untamed wildness, we may find ourselves once again inspired to live with the abandon of our forebears.

What We Will Be Has Not Yet Been Made Known.[1]

When I breathe my last breath, I anticipate joining God in the afterlife.

As you can imagine, I don't really know what that means. They are words. They are my attempt to speak about that which cannot be spoken. I no longer have a blow-by-blow account of how things will unfold. I don't know what I will be in the afterlife, or if I will even be Doug. It is a great mystery.

I imagine the afterlife the way I imagine being able to speak to an unborn baby. How would I prepare her for what's coming next? "Sweet child," I might say, "You are about to be born into a world of mountains and rivers, houses and trees. There is air to breathe, sunlight to warm your days and moonlight to comfort your nights. And, dear child, even though it seems to you that the whole world is dark, wet, and warm, you are already here in the world I am describing. You just can't see it yet."

The words we say to one another about the afterlife are as uncontainable as words about rocks and trees are to an unborn child.

When our scriptures speak of the end they use terms like "spiritual bodies" or "being clothed in the imperishable."[2] In truth, we have no idea what these words mean. Jesus spoke of life transcending body and brain,[3] but was vague enough that we don't really understand what he meant. Paul spoke of Jesus's resurrection in vague language, and suggested our destiny was the same as his.[4] But again, his words were an effort to speak about the unspeakable.

Vague, mysterious language is how Christians have best expressed our hopes for a transformed world, a transformed human experience, and the realization of God's profound and good purposes. Ours has always been a hope rooted in mystery and ineffable transcendence.

1. 1 John 3:2.
2. 1 Cor 15:44–57.
3. Mark 12:26–27.
4. Col 1:15.

Whatever our afterlife story ends up looking like, vague will be better than specific, abstract better than concrete.

My Afterlife

My own story of the Christian afterlife has had more stripped away than added in. The two-line story doesn't ring true anymore, but no concrete story has taken its place. I have a lot of questions. I wonder what consciousness might be like when it isn't being played in my brain's chemistry. I wonder what experience is like absent the chronology of moments I live in. I wonder what "one with God" means in experiential terms. What does "union with God" mean? I wonder if I will recognize "me" in any sense of me-ness.

My afterlife story is like the story of that unborn baby. My world is a warm and dark place. I just can't imagine mountains and trees and houses.

So I've stopped trying.

But though I do not have a specific or elaborate story, I do have a big hope, a big anticipation. I have a profound hope for the *something* Jesus suggested awaits us after we breathe our last breath.

I anticipate that after my last heartbeat, I will experience the mysterious resurrection into life that Jesus experienced. I just don't know what that means. Keeping mystery in Easter means keeping mystery in the afterlife, so I've just gotten comfortable with the ambiguity. To speak of life after life we have to use poetic language. Time before time began and time after time is over—these are constructs that don't lend themselves to anything but poetic, mythical, apocalyptic language.

So here I am, a child of my generation, living in a time in which many are abandoning the afterlife. And I am not.

Embracing the quantum worldview, I can't shake a sense of the interconnectedness and continuity that everything shares with everything. This was intuited by our Christian ancestors long ago. As a child of the quantum era, I can't shake it today. I have a deep sense of my continuity with God, a sense that it is in God that I live and move and have my being. I carry a deep sense of the indwelling, abiding spirit of Jesus. I walk with a sense of connectedness to others. I *feel* Paul's words, that we, being many, are one body, and that every one of us are members one of another.[5] When I read philosophers and physicists contend for the connectedness of everything, when I hear them speculate about human consciousness transcending the physicality of my brain, it resonates with my experience. It resonates with my Christian heritage. It informs my Christian story.

Something! Something Good!

My story of the afterlife is a story of something not nothing. And that something is good.

After I graduated seminary I borrowed my father-in-law's travel trailer and went to an abandoned horse ranch in central California to fast for forty days. My seminary years had been a tough go. Each class brought up more doubts, questions, and misgivings and I wasn't ready to stand up in front of people and tell them the kinds of things ministers tell people. I doubted prayer. I doubted the Bible. I doubted that humans could experience God. I doubted just about every Christian belief there is.

God bless my professors, patient as they were. For each objection, they gave a caring and reasoned response. However, try as they might, they could not help me shake my misgivings about the reliability of our faith.

And so, I went to the wilderness to fast.

In hindsight, I went with mixed motives. Part of me wanted to think of myself as a heroically spiritual man, the kind of man God favors. How silly was that? But a deeper part of me was chasing a yearning hunger for the experience of God. So I committed myself to the endeavor. I borrowed the trailer. I cleared things with the ranch owner. I told my wife I was going. I made the arrangements.

But by the seventh day I had run out of things to do.

Seven days doesn't sound like a long time when you've set aside forty, but when you're fasting and praying, seven days is an eternity! Only seven days in, and I had prayed every prayer I could think of to pray; I had done everything I could think of that fasting people do—and I'd done them all seven times.

5. Rom 12:5.

What had I been thinking?

My father-in-law had lent me a patch of artificial grass to roll out in the weeds in front of the trailer. On the seventh day, I was lying on this little oasis, looking up at the sky. With a bit of desperation, I said out loud: "God, what do I do now?"

Something unusual happened to me at that moment. As soon as those words came out of my mouth, other words began to bounce around in my head. I didn't hear a voice from heaven, nothing audible or dramatic. However, I experienced words in a way I don't normally experience them. The words that began to leap around inside me took me by surprise. "Study the compassion of Jesus." That's all. "Study the compassion of Jesus."

It's strange, I know.

With nothing else to do, I started to study. I studied everywhere in the scriptures where the words "Jesus" and "compassion" show up together. After two days, I had produced a ten page paper on Jesus and the Greek word "*splagchnizomai.*" The word means to have one's bowels turned over in deep compassion, sympathy, or concern for another. But after two days I was right back where I had been, worrying about what to do next, with thirty-one days to go.

I decided to do a Bible study technique I'd learned in college. The technique is to read a scripture story and then to imagine one's self in the story. The point is to imagine the details with as much specificity as possible: the weather, the smells, the sounds, and so forth. The idea is that imagination gives us access to a different part of the brain, and a deeper experience of the text.

So I lay down in the trailer to start imagining.

After a few texts, I came to the story of the widow of Nain.[6] In this story Jesus encounters a widow at the funeral procession of her son. She's doubly anguished. She has lost both husband *and* son, and on top of that, as a woman in a patriarchal society, faces financial insecurity as well. Seeing her in these desperate straits, Jesus's bowels are turned over with concern and kindheartedness toward her. He stops the procession, raises her son from the dead, and presents him back to her.

---

6. Luke 7:11–18.

That's the story. Next step, imagine. First I needed to determine whose experience I would imagine. If I were to project myself into the story, which character would I be? Not Jesus. Not the widow. How about the son? Okay. I've been a son before. I'll be him. So here I am, I imagined. I'm dead. I'm trying to imagine what it feels like to be dead. Okay. And now, I'm alive. I'm imagining what it feels like to be dead and then alive. I'm imagining what it feels like to see my mother cared for by this stranger. I'm imagining my gratitude for someone who has so profoundly intervened in my family's life.

And as I lay in that tiny trailer imagining, a terrible realization came crashing down on me. I saw something I had been hiding from myself for years.

I did not believe this story.

But it was not just the story I did not believe. I did not believe in a God that is good.

My mother had been a widow just like this woman was. *My* mother had experienced great pain just like this woman had. I had been a devout and good son, and had prayed to God to intervene in my mother's painful life. But no Jesus ever showed up to mitigate my mother's pain. No God interceded to alleviate her suffering. In fact, for years and years, despite my devout, faith-filled prayers, things had just gotten worse!

I became angry. What a crock! A good God? Like hell!

If God is good, if God's representative on earth is moved with compassion for widows, he had done a pretty good job keeping it hidden at my house!

In a moment of clarity I threw the Bible across the trailer. I said a few choice words and in an instant, made the determination that my Christian days were over. If I couldn't believe in a good God I had no business being Christian. It was a radical shift for a young man who had lived as devoutly as I had, but I made it without reservation. I realized that all the struggles I'd had in all those seminary classes were in fact just extensions of this one struggle. How could I believe *any* of this religious stuff if I couldn't believe in a good God?

On that day my world turned on a dime. I began to imagine my new, post-religious life. In the new world before me, I immediately had two regrets. First, I regretted having spent all that time and money getting a seminary degree. But just as quickly, it occurred to me that the current governor of California had a seminary degree, so I began to plan my new career in politics.

My second regret was for my wife. She had married a man who was going to be a minister. She *wanted* to be a minister's wife. Now she wasn't even married to a Christian man! I felt bad for her. But what could I do? I made some plans to help her through her disappointment, and it was settled.

My fast was over. My life had changed direction. I was ready to leave.

But I had no car.

I had towed the trailer out to the ranch and left my wife with the car. She came out every few days to bring me some juice boxes. So I was trapped. She was due to come out the next morning so my new life had to wait a day. With nothing to do until she arrived, I went to bed early. I determined that when she arrived the next day, I'd tell her the bad news and be off to my new life as an agnostic politician.

As I lay down to sleep, I felt a small impulse to be sure I'd covered all my bases. I prayed one last prayer. "God," I prayed, "out of respect for the last thirty years together, I'll give you until tomorrow morning to show me something I don't see. Otherwise, I walk away tomorrow and won't look back."

Because I'd gone to sleep so early, I awakened before five in the morning. I took a quick inventory to see if anything had changed. Nothing had. So I sat down to wait for my new life. To fill the time and give God every chance, I picked up a book that purported to answer the question of God's goodness in the face of human suffering.[7] I'd read it before. There was nothing in it for me.

My wife didn't arrive in the morning as expected. In fact, she didn't arrive until late that evening. So I kept reading. I kept sitting. I kept waiting.

At about ten-thirty in the morning, another strange thing happened to me.

I began to see pictures in my head. These were not visions; they were memories. But they were not memories the way I have memories. They unfolded in real time. If the episode I was remembering took five minutes, it felt like the memory itself took five minutes. It was like I was watching them on a screen in my head, more vividly, intensely, and lucidly than I have ever had memories. And these were not good memories. They were awful. I recalled in painful detail some family incidents that had occupied my prayers through my

7. Lewis, *Problem*.

teens and twenties; they were graphic and dreadful. They flooded through my mind for the better part of an hour. And as they unfolded, something happened to me.

Deep inside, I came to *know* that God is good.

I am fully aware this makes no sense. How could awful memories, memories in which God stood by and did nothing as my family suffered, how could these memories elicit a sense of God's goodness? It makes no sense.

But that is what happened to me.

In the period of less than an hour, there was inserted into my soul an unshakable conviction that stands to this day. God is good. I am safe.

God Is Good. I Am Safe

For centuries, this has been the testimony of those who deeply experience the spiritual life. However, it was not until that day that they were anything more to me than someone else's pretty words. You can understand why. Look around! A good God contradicts logic and the nightly news.

As we've seen, the three ideas of God's omnipotence, omniscience, and goodness can't coexist. That's why we have to hold our anthropomorphic images of God lightly. On the day God's goodness took such deep root in my soul, the only metaphors I had for God were anthropomorphic. Consequently, my conviction about God's goodness simply had to override the problems inherent in the metaphor. My experience was powerful enough to do that. That day, I began living in a dilemma. I had no logical construct for talking about it, but God's goodness had become an unshakable belief.

I trace this *rethinking-our-story* project back to that experience. When I became a minister twenty-five years ago, I knew the church was ill. However, for years I thought the problem could be solved by changing our practices. I thought if we were more spiritual, virtuous, relational, honest, trustworthy, or some such thing, we could solve our troubles. But each year I lived in the "*God-is-good, I-am-safe*" world, the more our cherished Christian story didn't work. I embarked on this project because at so many points, our current narrative directly undercuts the idea that God is good. My experience became more real to me than the traditional telling of our story.

God is good. I am safe.

That changes everything. It especially challenges the two-line story of the afterlife.

It challenges the dual narratives that consume our society: despair and the craving after stuff.

The Christian story is a beautiful story. It is a story our world needs.

The Christian story is a hopeful story, a story with a happy ending.

The task facing Christians today is to rethink our story deeply enough that it can once again be a gift of good news for our world. If we get it right, it is a direct challenge to the dark narratives that so wound us.

As Christians, we need a better story than a two-line afterlife. And it is ours to have. We need not anticipate standing before an angry or punitive God at a grand and final judgment. We need not spend our lives making sure we end up on God's good side. Not at all. Death has no sting. The gospel really *is* good news. Life wins. Love wins. Goodness prevails.

The specifics remain vague, hazy, mysterious, and unknown. But it is a story informed by hope.

A Story of Redemption

Our Christian story begins with the refrain, "it is good," "it is good," "it is good." Goodness has continued to reverberate through the generations. In the Christian story, our individual lives unfold in this matrix of goodness. Yes, the sin wound hurts us, but divine goodness is always there, always inviting us, always calling us, always healing and restoring us. Likewise, in our collective story, history unfolds in the same matrix of goodness. Yes, the planet has been wounded. Yes, sin and pain hold sway and dictate terms. But our story ends well. Love and life are not vanquished. Goodness prevails. God wins.

When something good gets broken, we fix it. Redemption is our God's way. Ours has always been a story of healing, growth, and the restoration of goodness, truth, and beauty.

That is our story.

With "eternity in my heart"[8] I look to a future of ever-deepening experience of the love and goodness that began our story. Whatever the afterlife holds, it is good. We are safe.

8. Ecclesiastes 3:11.

Afterword

18

Can We Still Be Christian?

So can we? Can we still be Christian in the quantum era? Sure we can.

However, we cannot be *Enlightenment Christians* in the quantum era.

Well, that's not true. We could. The Amish are still up there in Pennsylvania living out a Christian story that worked before Newton. So sure, we could *not* retell the Christian story for the quantum world. But if we would like to remain both Christian *and* citizens of our world, we have to rethink our story. And this could be one of the best things that could happen to us.

Throughout this book we have returned again and again to the Christian doctrine of ineffability. God, the spiritual, the transcendent—these simply cannot be contained in our minds, words, or experience. We see through a dark glass. We see shimmers, hints, and indicators of a reality that is beyond us. However, we cannot contain it.

Also, we've seen again and again how the quantum era invites us to return to this central doctrine of our faith. And this is a good thing! Perhaps it is the *best* thing for us.

The doctrine of ineffability helps us to approach the Bible both receptively *and* skeptically. It helps us step back from some of the intractable problems that are suffocating our faith, and explore our ancient truths more deeply. It helps us rethink our images of God in ways that lead us into a more robust spirituality. The doctrine is especially helpful when we rethink Jesus, the human being, and human nature in general. Ineffability allows us to imagine the unimaginable: that we carry within our very selves, the same *imago Dei* that Jesus carried, the presence and image of the Divine.

This ancient doctrine's time has come!

Ineffability allows us to navigate the quantum era. It allows us to be Christian in a universe that is relative, uncertain, and illusory. It allows us to tell *many* salvation stories. It allows us to imagine *many* ways we are saved. Ineffability allows us to step back from the punitive, hypocritical God implied by Anselm-Niagara. It gives us stories that help us once again hear the good news, the God-is-love narrative. When we embrace the ineffable, our two-line story of the afterlife doesn't remain the one and true story, and we don't have to live under the burdens it imposes on us.

This is good—very good!

Thank God for the quantum era!

The quantum era, and the recovery of our ancient doctrine of ineffability are not just allowing us to *remain* Christian. They are inviting us to be Christian with a health and verve we haven't enjoyed for over a hundred years. They are inviting us into a new reformation, another revival, another awakening. This is the best thing that could be happening to us. We're sick. History is inviting us back to health and well-being.

This book is an invitation to work with the season. It is an invitation to re-think, to go back to our churches, book clubs, Sunday classes, and coffee clutches, and take up the task of rethinking our story for our children and for this new era. It is an invitation to join together, shed our fears, and follow God's indwelling spirit into new stories, new interpretations, and new ways of talking about our spiritual lives.

Finally, I'll offer one last thought about how wild this journey could be.

Again, God is ineffable. Again, the word "God" is only a code word for speaking of Ultimate Reality. Again, we cannot speak of the unspeakable Divine. But again, when we try, we produce some of the most beautiful words ever spoken.

This being so, and with history knocking so insistently on our door, how far can we go? *How much* tinkering can our storytelling sustain and still be Christian?

Let's strip storytelling down to its most rudimentary elements and ask that: how far? When we tell stories, the most basic unit we use is the sentence. Hammered out early in human experience, it even predates our spiritual quest. In this basic structure, there is a subject and a verb. Or, there is a subject, verb, and object. This primitive construct tells a story about somebody (subject) doing something (verb) to somebody (object). I see you. God loves you. Time changes us.

There it is—storytelling and meaning-making in its simplest form.

Somebody does something to somebody.

Through most of our history, when we tell the story of God, we have always made him the noun, the subject or object. Either *God* does something to somebody, or somebody does something to God. Ultimate Reality does things, acts this way or that, and performs the actions that nouns perform.

That's how we've always told it. God is always the noun. But of course, we have also always wanted to tell our stories better and better. So we invented another part of language: the modifier. As soon as we have a noun, our minds automatically begin to wonder what kind of noun it is. What are the attributes of this noun? Is it a happy noun? A sad one? An angry noun? A patient and forgiving one? A great deal of Christian theology has been an attempt to tell a better story by coming up with the right adjectives to modify our noun-God. What kind of God do we have? What are his attributes? Is he changeable or unchangeable? Does he get angry or is he always patient? Is he just or is he merciful?

But ineffability allows us step back from this deeply ingrained interpretive habit. Sure, we've always done it that way, but we are in a new time. We are being invited to re-embrace our unknowable, unknown God. The quantum era affords us a great deal of storytelling latitude.

So let's strip this thing down and try it out. What happens if we tell our story with God as the verb instead of the noun? What if God is the action word in our lives? This, not being the way we've always done it, throws our mental constructs into a tizzy. Even our language gets tortured by the exercise. We often end our verbs with "-ing." We don't have language to speak of "God-ing."

But we could. We could make up some words to help us rethink our story. We could make up some words to help us be Christian in the quantum era.

The Fruit of the Divine Spirit, our tradition has always told us, is love, joy, peace, patience, kindness, goodness, faithfulness, gentleness, and self-control.[1] Again, we don't know what we are actually talking about when we speak of "God's Spirit," but through the centuries, when we try to describe our experience of the Divine these words keep coming up. When God-movement is happening, love is happening. When the God-wind is blowing, peace and patience are blowing. When God-action is in play, goodness and faithfulness are in play.

What if we speak of that which is unspeakable in *verb-God*, rather than *noun-God* terms? What if we imagine a story in which, when loving is happening, God-ing is happening. When peacemaking or wisdom-speaking is happening, God-ing is happening.

History is inviting us to set our imaginations free. It is inviting us to rethink our story, which in turn will change what we look for on the spiritual journey. And as we've seen, we *find* what we look for.

We have a deep hunger for Ultimacy, for the Divine. It comes hardwired into our humanity. In the past, we serviced this hunger with discussions about the attributes of our noun-God. The action parts of our religion tended to get afterthought status. Only after we figured out what our noun-God required of us were we free to embark on the action parts of our faith. Of course, good deeds have always been part of our Christian story. However, growing up in church, I always learned of them as *extra* things we did *after* we finished the noun-God disciplines. We read the Bible to hear what noun-God said. We listened to sermons about how noun-God wanted us to live. We said prayers to converse with noun-God. After all that was finished, *then* we were free to go out and do the good works noun-God asked of us.

But what if experiencing the Fruit of the Spirit is *actually* the experience of the Divine? What if giving and receiving love, is in fact, the experience of God? What if giving and receiving kindness and goodness, or practicing courage and generosity are actually experiences of verb-God? Ineffability allows us to imagine our Christian story in all kinds of different ways.

1. Gal 5:22–23.

We find what we look for. If we let our story run wild, we might find God in the simple experience of love, or peacemaking, or patience-having. If we look for God-ing in our loving, we will find it. If we look for God-ing in our reconciling or forgiving, we will find what we look for.

We find what we look for. A new story is an invitation to look for better things.

We *can* be Christian in the quantum era, but we cannot be Enlightenment Christians in the quantum era. We *can* be Christian in the quantum era, but we cannot remain locked in the confining story we hammered out during in the old worldview.

But that is not bad news. It is good!

New ways of telling our story open us to new ways of experiencing God— and Jesus, and the Bible, and salvation. New ways to tell our story help us look for new things, and to find what we look for.

The quantum era is a good thing for us.

A relative, uncertain, illusory universe is a good thing for us.

Recovering our ineffable center is a good thing for us.

We are Christians. We have a beautiful story. This new era is inviting us to recover it. This new era is inviting us to deepen our experience of God, Jesus, salvation, and our ancient spirituality.

This is good news.

This is a good story.

Bibliography

Augustine, St. *On the Trinity*. New York: New City Press, 1991.

Barna, George. *The Second Coming of the Church*. Nashville: Thomas Nelson, 1998.

Bernstein, Alan E. *The Formation of Hell: Death and Retribution*. Ithica: Cornell University Press, 1993.

Buechner, Frederick. *Beyond Words: Daily Readings in the ABC's of Faith*. New York: HarperCollins Publishers Inc., 2004.

Campbell, Ginger. "A Discussion of Consciousness: A Brief Introduction to Philosophy of Mind." Brain Science Podcast (2007). No Pages. Online: http://ec.libsyn.com/p/4/6/5/465b93abc5bfd30e/5-brainscience- Consciousness.pdf?d13a76d516d9dec2 0c3d276ce028ed5089ab1ce3dae902ea1d01cf803 fd6ce5ef071&c_id=1520864.

Campbell, Joseph. The Hero's Journey: Joseph Campbell on His Life and Work. New York: Harper & Row, Publishers Inc., 1990.

Chalmers, David J. "Consciousness and its Place in Nature." Philosophy Program; Research School of Social Sciences; Australian National University. Online: http://consc.net/papers/nature.pdf.

———. "Facing Up to the Problem of Consciousness." Philosophy Program; Research School of Social Sciences; Australian National University. Online: http://consc.net/papers/facing.pdf.

Craddock, Fred B., et al. *Craddock Stories*. Danvers MA: Chalice Press, 2001.

D'Souza, Dinish. *Life after Death: The Evidence*. Washington DC: Regnery Publishing, 2009.

Goodreads. "Pascal Quote." No pages. Online: http://www.goodreads.com/quotes/10567-there-is-a-god-shaped-vacuum-in-the-heart-of.

Grensted, L.W. *A Short History of the Doctrine of the Atonement*. Manchester: Manchester University Press, 1920.

Harris, Marvin. *Cows, Pigs, Wars, and Witches: The Riddles of Culture*. New York: Random House, 1974.

Higgins, Gregory. *Christianity 101: A Textbook of Catholic Theology*. Mahwah NJ: Paulist Press, 2007.

Hood, Jason. "The Cross in the New Testament: Two Theses in Conversation with Recent Literature (2000-2007)." WTJ 71 (2009) 281–95. Online: http://files.wts.edu/uploads/images/files/71.2.Hood.The%20Cross%20in%20the%20New%20Testament.pdf.

Hope, Jenny. "Near-death patients do see afterlife." Daily Mail (May 24, 2009). No pages. Online: http://www.dailymail.co.uk/health/article-24509/Near-death-patients-afterlife.html.

Jackson, Frank. "Epiphenomenal Qualia." Philosophical Quarterly, 32 (1982), 127–36. Online: http://instruct.westvalley.edu/lafave/epiphenomenal_qualia.html.

Julian of Norwich, "Quotations: God our Mother." No pages. Online: http://www.gloriana
.nu/mother.htm.

Kielberger, Craig, and Marc Kielberger. *Me to We: Finding Meaning in a Material World.*
New York: Fireside, 2006.

King Jr., Martin Luther. "I've Been to the Mountaintop." No pages. Online: http://www
.americanrhetoric.com/speeches/mlkivebeentothemountaintop.htm.

Kretzmann, Paul E. *The Kretzmann Project: Roman Government and Tax Collection in
Palestine. 1924. No pages. Online:* http://www.kretzmannproject.org/MAT/roman
%20government.htm.

Leaver, Rev. Dr. Richard G. *"Celtic Christianity."* No pages. Online: http://www.gbgm-
umc.org/journey/articles/celtic.htm.

Lewis, C. S. *Mere Christianity.* New York: HarperCollins, 1952.

———. *The Lion, the Witch, and the Wardrobe.* New York: HarperCollins Children's
Books, 1950.

———. *The Problem of Pain.* New York: Macmillan, 1962.

Markquart, Edward, "Astonished and Astounded." No pages. Online: http://www.sermons
fromseattle.com/easter_astounded.htm.

Merton, Thomas. "Taken from Modern Spirituality Series." Page 2–3. Online: http://
theliberatingsecret.org/reading_room/merton/pdf/Modern%20Spiritual%20Series
.pdf.

Nagel, Thomas. "What Is It Like to Be a Bat?" The Philosophical Review LXXXIII, 4
(October 1974) 435–50. Online: http://organizations.utep.edu/portals/1475/nagel_
bat.pdf.

Newell, J. Phillip. *Christ of the Celts: The Healing of Creation.* San Francisco: Jossey-Bass,
2008.

———. *The Book of Creation: An Introduction to Celtic Spirituality.* Mahwah NJ: Paulist
Press, 1999.

O'Callaghan, Jeffrey. "The Imagineer's Chronicles: Explaining the 'Reality' of Quantum
Superposition." No pages. Online: http://www.theimagineershome.com/blog/?p=
8587.

Perriman, Andrew. *Hell and Heaven in Narrative Perspective.* Posts on hell and life after
death from www.postost.net. 2012.

Randrup, Alex. "Idealist Philosophy: What is Real?" No pages. Online: http://philsci-
archive.pitt.edu/1216/1/reality.html.

Ring, Kenneth. *Mindsight: Near-Death and Out-of-Body Experiences in the Blind.* Palo
Alto, CA: William James Center for Consciousness Studies, 1999.

Rohr, Richard. *Things Hidden: Scripture as Spirituality.* Cincinnati: St. Anthony Press,
2008.

Saxon, David. "Interacting with Evangelical Scholarship: Lessons from the Niagara
Fundamentalists (1875–1900)." Online: http://www.dbts.edu/pdf/macp/2007/Saxon,
%20Interacting%20with%20Evangelical%20Scholarship.pdf.

Schihl, Dr. Robert. "The Immaculate Conception of Mary." No pages. Online: http://www
.ewtn.com/faith/teachings/maryc3a.htm.

Shushan, Gregory. *Conceptions of the Afterlife in Early Civilizations: Universalism,
Constructivism and Near-Death Experience.* New York and London: Continuum,
2009.

Thurman, Howard. *Jesus and the Disinherited. Boston:* Beacon Press, (1976).

Tippet, Krista. *"The Need for Creeds: An Interview with Jaraslov Pelikan." On Being with Krista Tippet* (October 2009). No pages. Online: http://www.onbeing.org/program/need-creeds/transcript/1291.

Van Lommel, Pim, et. al., "Near-death experience in survivors of cardiac arrest: a prospective study in the Netherlands." Lancet 358 (2001) 2039–45. Online: http://profezie3m.altervista.org/archivio/TheLancet_NDE.htm.

Williams, Kevin R. "An Analysis of Near-Death Experiences of Atheists." No pages. Online: http://www.near-death.com/experiences/atheists01.html.

Made in the USA
Columbia, SC
18 November 2020